Merchants of Williamsburgh

Merchants of Williamsburgh

Frederick C. Havemeyer Jr.
William Dick
John Mollenhauer
Henry O. Havemeyer

Harry W. Havemeyer

Merchants of Williamsburgh
Copyright © 1989, 2022 by Harry W. Havemeyer

Printed in the United States

ISBN-978-0-9854452-4-9

Contents

Merchants of Williamsburgh 2022

In the spring of 2022 my daughter Catherine and I have produced a paperback edition of *Merchants of Williamsburgh,* the story of the Havemeyers, Dicks, and Mollenhauers who settled in America in the nineteenth century and engaged in the business of refining sugar in Brooklyn. Additional photographs have been added, a few minor errors corrected, and a new final chapter brings the story of the waterfront sugar industry up to date. Otherwise, I have largely left the text as it was written in 1988, with the epilogue that reflected on the state of decay found in Williamsburgh at that time. Much has changed in the intervening years. In 2005 the city rezoned the waterfront of Williamsburgh, ushering in a building boom that has made the neighborhood a very desirable place to live. Restaurants and shops have flourished and the streets teem with young New Yorkers.

Harry W. Havemeyer
May 2022

Author's Notes
and Acknowledgments

In the following account I have chosen to use the German spelling of the Kingdom and the City of Hannover rather than the English version with a single *n* most often seen in English-language material today. I have also used the original spelling of Williamsburgh, the final *h* of which was dropped officially after the city's consolidation into Brooklyn in 1855. The name *Brooklyn* is the Americanized version of the name of the Dutch village Breuckelen, given to the new settlement in 1646 by the first Dutch immigrants to New Netherlands in the New World.

In compiling this story I have been greatly helped by three institutions, the collections of which have provided me with much valuable historical information. These are the New York Public Library, the New-York Historical Society, and the Brooklyn (formerly Long Island) Historical Society.

I would like to express my gratitude to three persons without whose assistance I would have been severely handicapped. William Dick's and John Mollenhauer's great-granddaughter, my cousin Direxa Dick Dearie, was an enormous source of help because she shared with me many records and papers about our great grandparents that are in her possession, and also because of her great enthusiasm for my project. Ruth Pasquine was my right hand, typing into her computer the final manuscript after successfully interpreting my longhand versions many different times. Finally, my wife, Genie Havemeyer, was my stylistic editor; her patience and skill in reading and improving the text have made the final version more readable. I am greatly in the debt of all three.

April 1988

Introduction

During the period of rapid industrial expansion in the United States following the end of the Civil War, many fortunes were made and lost. Manifest destiny was carrying people westward to search for new places to settle, to develop, and to populate. Railroads were being created all over the country. Oil wells were being dug and large factories were being built to make iron and steel. Small villages were becoming towns and small towns cities, almost overnight. This rapid industrialization followed and mirrored in many ways the Industrial Revolution in England. It required ingenuity, capital, and a willing work force. Lacking any one of these factors, it would not have occurred. This expansion was fueled in large measure by immigration from the Old World. From the 1840s on, and particularly after the Civil War, people from Ireland, Germany, Poland, and Italy were coming to the United States in increasing numbers, looking for work and opportunity for themselves and their families. This period has been written about very thoroughly by many authors and does not bear repeating except to set the background for the story to follow.

Three immigrants came from Germany to New York during the nineteenth century, one of those by way of London, England. The first arrived very early in the century (1802); the other two came around the middle (1845 and 1850). Each one was young and unmarried when he came to America. Each was the youngest son in a large family (two were orphans), and each was quite poor when he arrived. One had learned a trade as an apprentice, but the other two had only their heads and hands and a willingness to learn and to work hard. Each was thrifty and must have recognized the need for saving as a key to advancement. Each married in the New World and sired children who would follow in his footsteps. There is certainly nothing unusual about any of this among immigrants in the United States at any time; in fact it is a common story.

What is unusual is that the paths these three chose to follow became intertwined in such interesting ways. They came together because the trade they chose to pursue in the New World was the refining of cane sugar, and the locale for this endeavor was in due course to be a mile of waterfront along the East River in New York harbor known as Williamsburgh.

The three immigrants were Frederick Christian Havemeyer, William Dick, and John Mollenhauer. What follows is the story of Havemeyer's son and grandson and their involvement with William Dick and John Mollenhauer in sugar in Williamsburgh for fifty years. All four men were central to the development of a major industry in the time of industrial expansion in the United States, an industry that would get much notoriety and that would change a small village into a huge factory-dominated city. They knew each other well; their families eventually intermarried; and this author is a great-grandson of three and a grandson of the fourth.

To begin their story we must go back in time to Germany, whence it all began.

Merchants of Williamsburgh

1

The Old World
(1692-1866)

The land in the most northwestern part of what we know to-day as West Germany is rich, flat lowland, swampy in parts but generally well suited for most agricultural products, especially for potatoes, sugar beets, and their natural adjunct, a livestock industry. Bounded on the west by the Weser River, on the east by the Elbe River, and fronting onto the North Sea, the area has historically combined agriculture and shipping. The river ports of Bremen and Hamburg have played large roles from the time they were so-called free cities—that is, not under the control of any state or principality. To the south, Hannover became the capital city of the area. It has always been a prosperous part of Europe, and because of its proximity to the North Sea, a strategically critical part of Germany. The people of this land have been primarily of the Lutheran tradition. Although part of the Holy Roman Empire from earliest times, they were drawn to the reformed faith as espoused by Martin Luther from the early sixteenth century onward.

Hannover first became a distinct political entity in 1692 when the Duke of Brunswick, Ernest Augustus, was raised to the rank of Elector and his lands became known as the Electorate of Hannover. He was married to Sophia, granddaughter of James I of England, and because of this connection, their son was called to become King George I of England in 1714, the first of the Hannoverian kings of England. From the death of Ernest Augustus until 1837, the kings of England and the Electors of Hannover were one and the same. Hannover was under the protection of the British crown and prospered for almost a century until it was overrun by Napoleon during his conquest of Europe. Although this conquest brought political domination to Hannover, Napoleon introduced many of the civil liberties he had won in France; by creating a uniform code of laws, he planted the seeds of nationalism that flowered later under Bismarck.

In 1815 the Congress of Vienna reorganized Europe following the defeat of Napoleon. As part of that settlement, the former Electorate of Hannover became the Kingdom of Hannover, one of the loose confederation of thirty-eight states that made up what was known as Germany at that time. The British king remained the Hannoverian king. By 1830, a few of these "German" states won limited constitutions from their monarchs or dukes. The seeds sown in Britain and France were bearing fruit in Germany and Italy as well. Economic forces were also at work bringing about loose confederations of interest. In 1834 seventeen German states entered a custom union, or Zollverein, a sort of forerunner to the European Common Market today.

However, in 1837 a setback occurred in Hannover. England's King William IV died that year and was succeeded by Queen Victoria. Hannoverian law would not permit a woman monarch. The crowns separated and the fifth son of George III, Prince Ernest Augustus, Duke of Cumberland, became King of Hannover. An extreme reactionary and a violent anti-Catholic, he rescinded the limited constitution and ruled as an absolute monarch until his death in 1851. Only during the period 1848-49 was his rule threatened at all.

The period 1840 to 1848 was one of growing nationalistic feeling and liberal agitation. In 1848, revolution swept through much of Europe. In February, barricades were put up in the streets of Paris, the Citizen King Louis Philippe was overthrown, and the second French Republic established. France had again led the way in a successful revolution, and all monarchs throughout Europe felt threatened. Karl Marx had joined in this success, having just published with his partner, Friedrich Engels, the classic work *The Communist Manifesto*. In the German city of Frankfurt, one month later, liberals organized the Frankfurt Assembly, drafting and publishing a constitution for the German states.* The Frankfurt Assembly failed to impose the constitution on many of the German states (Hannover accepted it for only one year) and collapsed at the end of 1849. Only in France was the Revolution of 1848 successful, and as so often happens, it was followed by a period of extreme conservatism and repression, especially in Germany.

Meanwhile, during that revolutionary year of 1848, a struggle between Denmark and the German Confederation was taking place for control of the two duchies of Schleswig and Holstein. Lying to the south of Denmark and to the north and east of Hannover, Schleswig and Holstein had historically been independent and under the control of their own dukes. The population was largely Germanic and therefore resisted efforts made by Denmark from time to time to incorporate them. In 1848, King Frederick VII of Denmark declared the complete union of Schleswig and Holstein with his country. Revolution broke out in both duchies, and the German Confederation, including Hannover, came to their aid. Fighting continued on and off until 1850, when a peace treaty between Denmark and Prussia, the leader of the German Confederation, ended hostilities. Schleswig and Holstein remained apart from Denmark until 1866, when they were annexed into Germany.

The years of 1850 to 1866 in Hannover and in many other German states saw liberal sentiment disappear. Censorship and persecution followed. Hardest to bear was the knowledge of failure. The liberals had come so close to establishing a constitutional government that they became convinced that democracy could never thrive in Germany. Thousands emigrated to shape their lives in the New World—many, like Carl Schurz, to the United States. In Hannover, King Ernest Augustus had died in 1851 and was succeeded by his son King George V. To some extent his kingdom

---

* Among those German liberals was Carl Schurz (1829-1905), who later fled to the United States, where he became secretary of the interior, the most prominent perhaps of the liberal German immigrants to the New World.

was still under the protection of his cousin Queen Victoria, but time was growing short for "independent" Hannover. In Berlin to the east, plans were being made for the total unification of Germany by that master strategist of the nineteenth century, Otto von Bismarck.

Playing Austria, Russia, France, and Britain off against one another, expanding all the while the power of Prussia and its military might, Bismarck made his country and his king the major power in continental Europe. By 1866, the time was right to strike at Austria, and in six days he forced the surrender of the grand Hapsburg empire. With that victory, Prussia literally absorbed all the German states north of the Main River, including Hannover, whose king, George V, had made the fatal mistake of siding with Austria. Although he held his title until his death, the king of Hannover was now a puppet of the German Empire under William I and Bismarck.*

Five small towns are a part of our story. Four are in the old Kingdom of Hannover. The other, the town of Bückeburg, is in the neighboring principality of Schaumberg-Lippe, thirty miles west of the city of Hannover, near the Weser River. This town began as the seat of Prince Ernest von Schaumberg in 1619. It remained the capital of that independent principality for three centuries and was not integrated with Germany until 1918. The old Stade Kirche (town church) still stands. By 1660 it is recorded that the master baker of the town was one Hermann Hovemeyer. The family can be traced from then until the last years of the eighteenth century, when first William and then his brother, Frederick Christian, left Bückeburg for London and later for New York, the former arriving in 1799, the latter in 1802. They had changed their surname to Havemeyer.

In the tiny hamlet of Bruchhagen** on September 24, 1823,

---

* In 1871, following the defeat of France, William I was crowned Emperor of Germany in the palace of Versailles outside Paris.

** Bruchhagen is twenty miles north of Bückeburg and forty miles northwest of the city of Hannover.

Charles William Dicke was born. Lying a mile or so south of the village of Steyerberg in the parish of Schinna near Stolzenau in Hannover, Bruchhagen must have been a farming community on the west bank of the Weser River. We know that William had an older brother, John W. Dicke, who preceded him to America. William received a thorough education afforded by the schooling of that country. He remained with his parents as long as they lived; after they died, in 1845, at age twenty-two he came to America, following his brother. He also had dropped the *e* in the spelling of his surname. Also in Hannover, but twenty miles northeast of Bremen in Hanstadt near Zeven, on October 2, 1819, Anna Marie Vagts was born, the daughter of Claus and Christine Vagts. It is not known when Anna came to America, but on November 19, 1848, William and Anna were married in St. Matthew's Evangelical Lutheran Church on Walker Street in downtown Manhattan by the pastor C. F. E. Stohlmann. John W. Dick and Gerhardt Vagts witnessed the union of their brother and sister respectively. The newlyweds made their first home together at the corner of Chestnut and Oak streets in the City Hall area, living over their grocery store.

Thirty miles east of the port city of Bremerhaven in the old Kingdom of Hannover is found the small village of Ebersdorf and its neighbor Bremervorde, five miles away. These villages were the birthplaces respectively of John Mollenhauer and Dorothea Christina Gasina Siems. Mollenhauer, the youngest son in a farming family, was born on August 13, 1827. Siems, the younger daughter of Theodore and Julia Siems, was born on April 9, 1830. It is likely that they had known each other in Germany, as their homes were only a few miles apart.

The first fourteen years of John's life were spent on his father's farm. He then served a five-year apprenticeship with a dealer in general merchandise. At the end of that period, he stayed on as a junior clerk for an additional year and a half. In 1848 he served his country in the war against the Danish over Schleswig-Holstein, but after remaining in the army for twenty-two months, he expressed a desire to come to America, whereupon his former employer purchased him a substitute to serve while the war continued. Sailing from Germany in 1850, John Mollenhauer, then twenty three, landed in New York after a long sea voyage and found employment in a grocery store. Doris Siems (as she was then known) emigrated four years later. Shortly after her arrival in May 1854, they were married by Pastor Stohlmann in St. Matthew's Evangelical Lutheran Church, as the Dicks had been earlier. The Mollenhauers settled at first on Hester Street, near Eldridge Street, and then later moved uptown somewhat to 205 Third Avenue. Like William and Anna Dick, they lived above their grocery store. Why did Frederick C. Havemeyer, William Dick, and John Mollenhauer emigrate when they did? The reasons cannot now be known for certain, but suppositions can be made. Each was young and came from humble working people. It is said that Dick was penniless when he arrived in New York. Each was a younger son. Havemeyer and Dick were orphans; Mollenhauer had left older brothers in Germany. Dick's older brother had preceded him to New York, and William came after his parents had died. Each became a merchant in the New World. The Havemeyers were bakers in the Old. Mollenhauer was the son of a farmer, and it is likely that Dick as well was familiar with sugar beets and molasses. The 1840s and '50s were a period of large German immigration to the United States, as has been noted. Some came, like Schurz, to avoid political repression. Many others were of the merchant class, leaving their homeland in search of new opportunity. They would make their mark in investment banking, forming such great houses as Kuhn Loeb and Lehmann Bros. The breweries and sugar refineries tended to be dominated by the Germans as well. Like most immigrant people, German families settled near one another, belonged to the same churches, and often were buried in the same cemeteries. First-generation Germans did not assimilate easily. Language was a barrier, and discrimination, if not outwardly practiced, was always lurking in the background.

2

Sugar Refining in Manhattan
(1730-1865)

Sugar refining had existed on Manhattan Island since 1730, when Nicolas Bayard opened his "bakery." The sugar houses were small, were inland from the waterfront, and usually operated with as few as five or six men. They were known as "bakeries" because the sweet juice, having been clarified with ox blood, clay, and albumen, was baked for hours in a kettle to produce an off-white crystalline sugar loaf. The product was expensive and used largely by the wealthy, who broke off pieces of the loaf, held it between their teeth, and drank coffee through it. The sugar houses produced very small quantities of this sugar. Eight hundred pounds per day would have been a large output. Often the owners and laborers lived in or very near the "bakeries." Business must have been profitable, however, because many small houses had been started in lower Manhattan during the eighteenth century.

Old and prominent names were associated with sugar. Livingston, Bayard, Cuyler, Roosevelt, Stewart, and Van Cortlandt were some of the families with members who were either refiners or merchants. In 1763, for instance, Rhinelander built a sugar house near Rose, Duane, and William streets. On Pine Street, between Nassau and William streets, stood the house of Messrs. Edmund Seaman & Company. It was this firm that in 1799 engaged a new sugar boiler, William Havemeyer, freshly trained in London, to manage its refinery.

London was the most advanced sugar refining center in the world in 1800, the best place to gain apprenticeship in the craft. William and later his younger brother Frederick had gone there from Bückeburg to learn the skills of the business. Apprenticeship over, William—and a few years later, Frederick—came to New York. William entered the employ of Messrs. Seaman & Company. Frederick is listed in the New York directory as a baker at 27 Dey Street in 1804. On April 10, 1805, they leased a plot of land at 87 Vandam Street from Trinity Church on which to build a new sugar house. It opened for business on January 1, 1807, under the name of Wm. and F. C. Havemeyer. The following year it was expanded by the addition of the adjoining lots. By 1810, the firm's address was 87, 89, and 91 Vandam Street. The building was two stories high, and three hired men, in addition to the two owners, were employed. Daily production was four thousand pounds, mostly of loaf sugar. Soon new forms of sugar were sold: crushed sugar, powdered sugar, and some granulated sugar. This, the original Havemeyer sugar refinery, continued to operate on Vandam Street until the mid-1850s, by which time it had become obsolete and a new technology had been developed to refine sugar.

The two Havemeyer brothers, having established themselves in business successfully, married and had families. William and his wife, Susannah Clegg, had four children, two of whom were sons. Frederick and his wife, Catherine Billiger, had eleven children, seven of whom were sons. The male children of both families remained in the sugar business, and by 1828 Frederick C. Havemeyer Jr., having attended Columbia College for two years, joined his cousin William F. Jr. to operate the Vandam Street refinery under the name of Wm. F. & F. C. Havemeyer Jr. This partnership continued until 1841, when both cousins left the firm in the hands of their respective brothers and invited William Moller, an experienced refiner, to join it. The new firm of Havemeyers & Mollers continued until 1856, when the Havemeyers sold their interest to the Mollers after the death of Diedrich Havemeyer, the younger brother of Frederick C. Havemeyer Jr. William Moller and his son continued to operate the firm until about 1876.

Meanwhile in London, great technological advances were taking place that would dramatically change the character of sugar refining. The vacuum pan, developed in 1812, would permit sugar to be crystallized much more rapidly, and because boiling could take place at less than 212° Fahrenheit (under vacuum), the crystals would not be burned or caramelized. They could be pure white. However, the vacuum pans required large amounts of water and steam. At the same time the use of bone black, made from animal bones, was adopted. The sugar liquor was filtered through it, resulting in the removal of all color from the granulated final product. No longer need sugar be dirty white. The filters and the kilns needed to revivify the char at those very high temperatures were huge and required much space and much fuel. The centrifugal machine was developed to separate the crystal from the molasses coating on it. This efficient way to remove solid impurities speeded the entire process but required much power. Lastly, the granulator, to dry the moist crystals by blowing hot air over them, was developed. These four technical developments revolutionized the industry. Modern sugar refining, born in London, spread to New York and other places. It required waterfront space, large amount of capital, and many workers. The first person in America to see this revolution and to act upon it was Frederick Christian Havemeyer Jr. (1807-1891), son of the immigrant father.

After leaving the sugar firm in 1841, William F. Havemeyer went into political life, later becoming mayor of New York. Frederick C. Jr., who also left the family firm, traveled extensively and otherwise pursued his education. It is known that he made several trips to Europe with parts of his family. Undoubtedly he went often to London as well, where he closely observed the new developments in the industry. He became an expert in the business, with a worldwide knowledge. By 1856 he was ready to return to sugar refining. With his son George W. Havemeyer and Dwight Townsend, another refiner, he leased a large warehouse on the waterfront on South Third Street in Williamsburgh, Brooklyn—the beginning of the first large modern sugar refinery in America. There is no doubt that by age forty-nine F. C. Havemeyer Jr. had become a pioneer in his country of a new industry. Following the lead of London, he had the vision that resulted in the formation of the Sugar Trust thirty-one years later. Once Havemeyer, Townsend & Company had built its sugar refinery in Williamsburgh, all in-land refineries became obsolete. This new refinery could produce more sugar per day (300,000 pounds in the beginning) than all the others could produce in a month. It could produce at much less cost, and the sugar was pure white, not brownish anymore. The *New York Times* said of F. C. Havemeyer Jr. at the time of his death (July 29, 1891):

> He was credited with doing more than anyone else to building the American sugar refining in-dustry and was considered the outstanding au-thority on refining.

In 1845 William Dick arrived in New York and joined his brother John W. Dick in a small grocery business on the Lower East Side of Manhattan. They were first located at the corner of Reade and Chestnut streets. By 1852 they had moved to 8 Oak Street, where William and Anna Dick also lived. In 1854, William Dick opened a flour and feed store at 167 West Street near Murray with a new partner, a man ten years his senior, Lur Wintjen.

Wintjen had been born in the Kingdom of Hannover in 1813. He had come to New York at the age of eighteen and found work in shipping. Somewhat later he was involved in the grocery trade as well. In 1846 he moved his residence to South Ninth Street in Williamsburgh, and in 1849 he married Margaretha Vagts, the younger sister of Anna Dick. It was very natural then for the two brothers-in-law to go into business together. It was also in 1854 that William and Anna Dick with their young son, John Henry, followed the Wintjens to Williamsburgh, locating briefly on South Tenth Street before moving to 77 Union Avenue, where their daughter Anna Margaretha was born and where they were to live for over ten years.

The partnership of Wintjen and Dick was in flour and feed for only four years. In 1858 they were joined by a third partner, an

Above, William Dick
(1823-1912). *Right*, John
Mollenhauer (1827-
1904). *Below*, Frederick C.
Havemeyer Jr. (1807-1891)

experienced refiner, Schumacher, and they built a small sugar refinery at the corner of 83 Pike Street and 207 Cherry Street, two blocks from the East River and under the shadow of the Manhattan Bridge of today. Their timing was poor, as in that year the large Havemeyer refinery opened on the Williamsburgh waterfront. Undaunted, they continued operating in that location for seven years, until 1865, when they acquired a large brick warehouse at the foot of Division Avenue on the Williamsburgh waterfront just to the south of the Havemeyer plant. They built their new refinery there in the warehouse.

It is interesting to observe that as early as 1854 William Dick was able successfully to manage a flour business and then a sugar business located in Manhattan while living in Williamsburgh. This was possible because of the numerous ferries that regularly crossed the East River by then. Even so, it was a very long commute from Union Avenue in Williamsburgh to Pike Street in Manhattan and later on to Wall Street, where the successor firm of Dick & Meyer had their offices.

John Mollenhauer, the farmer's son, was the last of the three to arrive in the New World, which he did in 1850. His first job, like Dick's, was that of a clerk in a grocery store on the Lower East Side of Manhattan at the corner of Hester and Eldridge streets. He lived over the store as well. After two years he had saved enough to go into business for himself, locating at 159 Walker Street just south of Canal Street. He and his new wife, Doris, continued to live over the store. The year 1860 saw a move into the wholesale wine and liquor business, with Mollenhauer's new store at 256 Cherry Street just up the street and a few blocks from the Wintjen and Dick refinery. Mollenhauer was very successful in this endeavor and was said to have made himself a fortune. In 1865 he decided to move his large family of five children to Williamsburgh and to retire from business. This was the first of three retirements in his life. A three-year trip back to the old country of Hannover followed, but when he returned to Williamsburgh, he decided to try his hand in sugar. He bought some land on Rush Street, a block away from his friend Dick's sugar house, built a molasses and syrup house, and opened his new business there in 1869.

After the end of the Civil War the stampede to Brooklyn started. Many others would join in. They chose the section of waterfront between Newtown Creek on the north and Wallabout Bay on the south. It had been the city of Williamsburgh, but by then it was a part of Brooklyn called the Eastern District.

Before looking at the period of intensive development of the sugar industry in the Eastern District, we should look at Williamsburgh's history and consider why in the second half of the nineteenth century it became the center of sugar refining in America.

A view of the East River from Williamsburgh in 1848.

3

Early Williamsburgh Prior to 1857

Williamsburgh, the part of Long Island that was to become the great center of industrial enterprise in the second half of the nineteenth century, was almost entirely unsettled in 1770. Dense thickets covered hundreds of acres of bog and lowland. It was known then as Cripplebush because the scrub oak, or cripplebush, dominated the land. During the American Revolution, British soldiers cleared the thickets for fuel, so that by 1800 much of the land was suitable for farming—primarily fruit and vegetables. The early farmers conveyed their produce to market in Manhattan by ferry from the terminal point at the foot of Metropolitan Avenue across the East River.

About the year 1800 a New Yorker, Richard M. Woodhull, began to acquire farms in this part of Long Island. A farm of thirteen acres lying along the shoreline and belonging to Charles Titus was bought by Woodhull in 1802. He then engaged his friend, a United States Army engineer named Colonel Jonathan Williams, to survey and lay out a settlement on the Titus farm. Woodhull called the settlement Williamsburgh in honor of his friend. Thus the area received the name by which it is known today. Another developer, Thomas Morrell, was acquiring farms in the area as well, and he started a second ferry to Manhattan from the foot of Grand Street. By 1811, Woodhull was experiencing difficulties in financing his new development, and he went bankrupt. After a sheriff's sale, the entire Woodhull speculation came under the control of Morrell. By 1814, Morrell is listed as owner of all the Williamsburgh lots and all the land between Newtown Creek and Wallabout Creek. The population of this area in 1814 was 759.

The first industrial enterprise in Williamsburgh, a distillery, was established by Noah Waterbury in 1819 at the foot of South Second Street (later part of the site of the Havemeyers & Elder refinery). Waterbury later became acknowledged as the "Father of Williamsburgh." He built a large house, known as the Waterbury mansion, on a site one block inland from his distillery; here he and his son, James M. Waterbury, lived until the late 1850s. They were among the most prominent and wealthiest men of the community. In the 1847 listing of the solid men of Williamsburgh, Noah Waterbury showed assets of $200,000, and his son James, of $175,000. Noah was an originator and first president of the Williamsburgh City Bank. James was a founder of the New York Yacht Club in 1844. Their yacht *Julia* was built by George Steers, brother of the builder of the yacht *America*. It was moored just south of their home in the Wallabout Creek. When the Havemeyer refinery moved to Brooklyn, to the South Second Street site, Waterbury moved his distillery to South Ninth Street. Much later, in the 1890s, his mansion was used to house laborers working at the nearby sugar plant.

In 1827, the village of Williamsburgh was chartered by the State of New York. Noah Waterbury was chosen its first president from among the five trustees, who included Thomas Morrell and Abraham Meserole. At that time the village included twenty-three farms. Its population was 1,007. The first map of the village, dated 1833, shows streets laid out in a rectangular grid and identified by number, with the exception of Grand Street. It was not until 1885 that names replaced numbers for those streets running north-south.* Streets running east-west are still numbered streets today, with few exceptions. Only a few of these streets actually existed in 1833, but the plan had been adopted.

Growth through the 1830s was gradual, not dramatic. The financial panic of 1837 and resultant depression affected Williamsburgh. Several of the small businesses closed, and the village

---

* For clarity I will refer to north-south streets with their post-1885 names.

trustees reconsidered the charter and deferred the plan to annex the new village of Bushwick to the east. A public meeting was called to investigate the debts and financial affairs of the village. Confidence gradually returned, however, and by 1840 there existed in Williamsburgh six churches, several schools, nine rope-walks (cordage), two shipyards, two tanneries, two distilleries, five hat factories, a glue factory, a carpet factory, and a fire insurance company. The population was listed as 5,094, a very lively village indeed.

During the 1840s the village of Williamsburgh began to take on the appearance of a town and then a city. The population grew to 35,000, and most of the projected streets were now opened. Several new ferries were established to Manhattan from a terminal at the foot of South Sixth and South Seventh streets. It was during this time that the main street came to be called Broadway (it had been South Seventh and South Sixth streets), a more desirable name to the town's people. The *Williamsburgh Times* of September 14, 1848, described the town as follows:

> Williamsburgh is a great place, it has all the elements of a great city, an astonishing touch of all the cardinal virtues with a corresponding number of vices to keep them in exercise. Though we have a sprinkling of rowdyism, we have many redeeming features that stand out in bold relief giving prominency to a character. With some of the best public schools in the State of New York, a fire department that "can't be beat" and some of the most interesting young ladies that can be found between Maine and Texas, we are brought to the conclusion that we are not to be sneezed at. On the bright side of the question we have thirteen places of worship, a Bible, a Tract, a Temperance and a Benevolent Society and four newspapers. On the dark side we have four hotels, two Bowling Saloons, several Billiard Tables and a bushel or two of politicians.

> We have just enough of poverty to preserve
> our benevolence from rust, sufficient influence
> to keep our inferiors, New York and Brooklyn,
> from disgracing the nation and patriotism in any
> quantity to keep up the Fourth of July as it should
> be kept. Our young ladies are not over fond of
> novel reading and our young men are not much
> addicted to smoking cigars. We have a splendid
> City Hall in perspective. Our aldermen are men
> of weight and our popular patriots are so eco-
> nomical that they will not allow "the upper ten" to
> pay anything to the public expenses.

James B. Wilson, an architect and builder, located his own home
on Kent Avenue and South Fifth Street. Of colonial architecture,
it was considered one of the finest buildings overlooking the river.
He built many of the most prominent public buildings in this
style, among them banks, churches and office buildings throughout Williamsburgh and Brooklyn. He died in 1909, at age nine-
ty-two.

The solid men of Williamsburgh 1847, referred to before, listed
forty-four names. Almost all of these names were of English or
Irish ancestry. There was not a German name among them. However, it is known that by the early 1840s in the easternmost part
of Williamsburgh, near Bushwick, a population of Germans had
settled. This community was called Dutchtown and was always
identified as a separate area in the same manner as we might iden-
tify East Harlem in Manhattan today. This was at the beginning
of the German immigration, and it was into this community of
Dutchtown, at 77 Union Avenue, that William and Anna Dick
moved in 1857, soon after they left Manhattan. By then the area
was well established and very distinctive. The center of Williamsburgh was still near the East River, extending three or four streets
inland and four or five streets north and south of Broadway. This
was not to change for many years to come.

As the decade of the 1850s opened, Williamsburgh had grown

to such an extent that its leaders wanted city status given to it. By the end of 1851, the state legislature in Albany had granted the necessary charter, and on January 1, 1852, the City of Williamsburgh was born. Dr. Abraham J. Berry was elected the first mayor. Dr. Berry, a physician, was a longtime resident and leading citizen. He was not, however, listed among the solid men referred to earlier. One must conclude that the remuneration of doctors was modest indeed at that time. The years 1851 to 1853 saw the founding of many institutions that carried on into the next century. Among them were the first savings bank in 1851 (The Williamsburgh Savings Bank; Samuel Meeker, president); the first commercial bank in 1852 (The Williamsburgh City Bank; Noah Waterbury, president); the first insurance company in 1853 (The Williamsburgh City Fire Insurance Company; Edmund Driggs, president); and the Mechanics Bank of Williamsburgh in 1853, a forerunner of the bank of which William Dick was later president.

During these years when Williamsburgh was an independent city, the German community was expanding but was still located in the Dutchtown area around Meserole Street, Scholes Street, and Montrose Avenue. A word should be said about Abraham Meserole, after whom the street was named and who was one of the five original Williamsburgh trustees. He was a descendant of Jean Meserole, a Frenchman who came to America in 1663 and cleared a farm of some hundred acres between the East River and Roebling Street. Jean Meserole died in 1695, but the farm remained in his family until 1800, when it was broken up. Some of it was sold to Charles Titus and some to Noah Waterbury. The Meseroles were the first owners of almost all of what became the center of Williamsburgh in the mid-nineteenth century.

In the German section on Meserole Street, a Turn Verein, a gymnastics club, was organized in 1853. The Turn Verein School adjoined the Turn Hall, a gymnasium, across the street. In the next block, the Williamsburgh Saenger Bund, a singing group, began in 1855. On neighboring Montrose Avenue, Edward F. Roehr started a German Masonic paper called *The Triangel*, which was

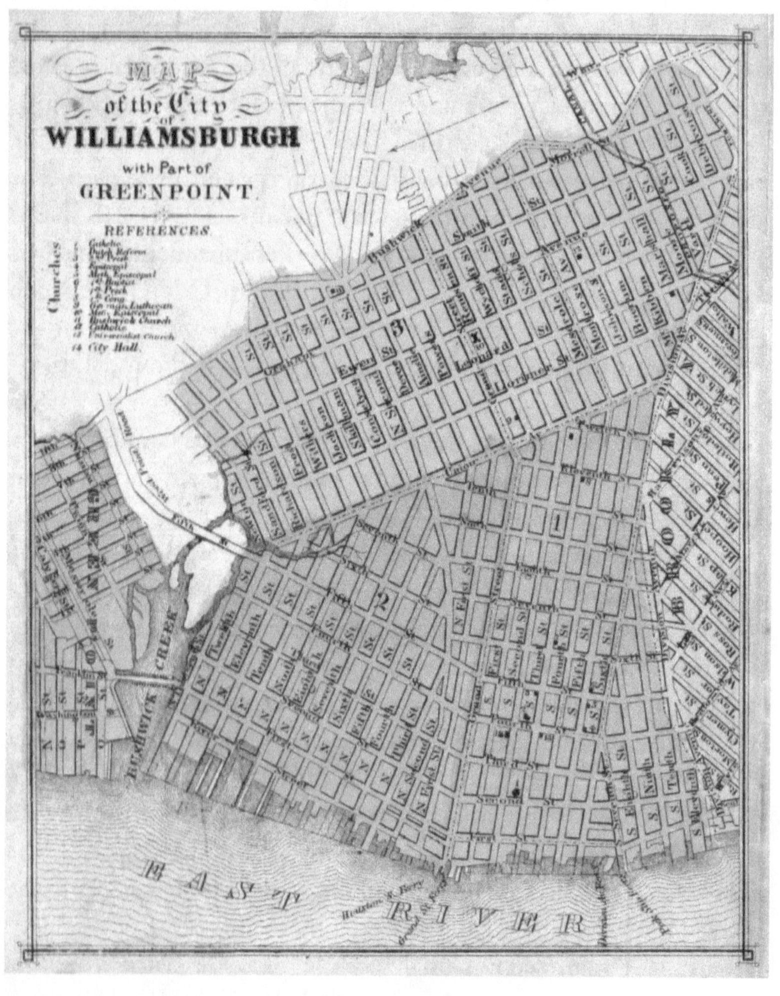

Map of the City of Williamsburgh in 1852.

published for twenty-five years before it became part of *The Long Islander*. Somewhat later in 1866, the German Savings Bank was founded at 84 Montrose Avenue. Finally, on Ten Eyck Street, St. John's German Evangelical (Lutheran) Church was started in 1853. This must have been a friendly, congenial community for the Dick family to have entered in 1857.

In 1854, William Wall succeeded Dr. Berry, Williamsburgh's first mayor, and became the second and last mayor. As much as ten years earlier, groups of citizens had begun discussing the possible consolidation of Williamsburgh with Brooklyn under a single city government. By 1855 the plan had been worked out. The city of Williamsburgh, with the adjoining areas known as Greenpoint to the north and Bushwick to the east, were all consolidated into the city of Brooklyn. Williamsburgh was called the Eastern District of that city. It had been a separate city for only three years—perhaps the shortest life span of any city in the country. Its population had grown by 1855 to 50,000, a figure that included a substantial number of Germans.* It was large enough to support the industrial enterprises that were about to be developed there. After the consolidation, Brooklyn became the third-largest city in America.

During the 1840s, several wealthy men had built mansions to join Noah Waterbury's. Along Kent Avenue, Abraham Meserole lived between South Third and South Fourth streets, and Samuel Hicks between South Sixth and South Seventh streets. William Wall, Abraham Berry, and Lawrence Waterbury had homes on "Colonnade Row," residences similar to those in Brooklyn Heights today. These were on what had been the Meserole farm with an unobstructed view down the river as far as Governor's Island. These were frame houses with columns on their porches in the Mount Vernon style. Also in this area along the river were the Williamsburgh Hotel and the Franklyn House.

---

* The population of Germans in Williamsburgh continued to grow during the years ahead until by 1890 they had become the largest ethnic group in all of Brooklyn. Valuing mutual support and familiar customs and speaking the same language, they transformed "old" Williamsburgh into a truly German city.

The Williamsburgh waterfront between Bushwick Creek on the north and Wallabout Creek on the south ran in a straight line north-south for a distance of a little more than a mile. The water along this mile was deep enough for the vessels of that time to dock at piers. In 1828, a street had been opened, called First Street, running along the entire length, and a thousand feet or so inland from the East River. Much later First Street was renamed Kent Avenue after Chancellor James Kent, a New York jurist. Prior to the 1850s, First Street looked very much the way a rural lane might look today. Early drawings of the area are pastoral, with a few houses on the high ground back from the water and a small ferry at a dock—most likely Woodhull's Metropolitan Avenue Ferry.

During the early 1850s there were only a few factories to spoil the residential neighborhood, such as Waterbury's distillery and the People's Steam Sugar Refinery, a small sugar house directly south of Waterbury's. There were also some ferry docks at South Seventh Street. Horse carts ran along Kent Avenue, providing local transport. By and large the waterfront was residential, and businesses were two or three blocks or more inland.

The mid-1850s marked the beginning of rapid change on the Williamsburgh waterfront. Good deep water, plenty of labor, and most important of all, space to build, were available. Those were the requirements Frederick C. Havemeyer Jr. was searching for in 1856 for his modern sugar refinery. He found them on South Third Street and Kent Avenue. However, his was not the first sugar house in Brooklyn. There had been a few small ones similar to those in Manhattan. Some produced molasses. Others, such as Crab & Wilson, where George R. Bunker* got his start with his uncle John Wilson, produced grape sugar, or glucose. Although not the first, the Havemeyers & Elder plant, opening in 1857 as Havemeyer, Townsend & Company, was to become the largest in the United States, ultimately producing over five million pounds

---

* See Chapter 5.

of sugar per day—the jewel in the crown of the Sugar Trust. By 1887 the Williamsburgh waterfront would no longer be residential at all. In that mile along the East River, seven large new sugar refineries would be operating and producing more than half of the sugar consumed in the entire country. It would become the largest manufacturing industry in Brooklyn, with an annual product in excess of $100 million.

Above, the original waterfront sugar refinery erected by Frederick C. Havemeyer Jr. at the foot of South Third Street, in 1858. Williamsburgh, Brooklyn. *Below*, a view of the same refinery, c. 1870.

4

The Coming of the Large Sugar Refineries (1857-1887)

The creation of a large concentration of sugar refineries did not happen immediately. In fact, during the first part of the thirty-year period 1857-1887, the only new refinery in the area was Havemeyer, Townsend & Company on South Third Street. Opened in 1857 with a capacity of 300,000 pounds per day, it became known in 1863 as Havemeyers & Elder. Dwight Townsend had left the firm and F. C. Havemeyer Jr. invited his son-in-law, Joseph Lawrence Elder, to join his son Theodore A. Havemeyer in partnership after his son George had been killed in a refinery accident in 1861. By 1868 Elder had died and Havemeyer's sons Thomas J. and Henry O. were added to the partnership, along with Havemeyer's nephew Charles H. Senff. The refinery itself now included most of the block from South Second to South Third Street, all of the block from South Third to South Fourth Street, and a good part of the block from South Fourth to South Fifth Street. A finger pier had been built to dock raw sugar cargoes at refinery property. By the early 1870s, refinery capacity exceeded one million pounds per day.

The need for labor, waterfront property, and space was mentioned earlier. The refinery process by this time began with raw sugar being shipped in large wooden casks in sailing vessels from the Caribbean (later in jute bags in steamships). Unloaded at pierside, the sugar was removed from the casks and melted with steam heat. The resultant liquor was mechanically clarified. Next, by passing it through huge filters filled with bone char, its color was adsorbed. This animal bone char was revivified for reuse by heating it to very high temperatures in what was known as the retort house. The sugar liquor, now pure white, was concentrated and then crystallized at temperatures of less than 212° F, in huge vacuum pans. The resultant crystals were then spun in a centrifugal machine to remove the coating of syrup and dried in large hot-air granulators before being packed in casks (later cotton bags). Finally, the sugar was transported by rail to customers throughout much of the country. A large labor force was needed, a thousand or more men to operate the day and night shifts and to handle the raw sugar at the waterfront. Industries related to refining, particularly cooperage and transportation, were needed close at hand, if not directly adjacent. Steam was also required in huge amounts, which meant a large boiler and power plant, together with a constant supply of coal.

To create such an endeavor in the 1860s and '70s required large amounts of capital. To find that capital required a record of success and a good profit margin on sugar sold, for retained earnings were almost the sole source of funds for expansion in those days. This partly explains why only the Havemeyer refinery was able to expand until 1870-71. There were other reasons, and to understand them one must briefly look at the United States sugar market during this period.

During the Civil War period, from 1861 to 1865, raw sugar was a scarce commodity, partly because transportation was lacking and partly because much of the sugar industry in the Gulf States was destroyed. Demand for sugar during this period was very low as well. In 1865, per capita consumption was only eighteen pounds per year, not conducive to a boom in trade. However, at the beginning of the 1870s, per capita consumption jumped to forty pounds per year. The price of sugar, reflecting the resultant shortage, rose dramatically, so that those who were still in the business and could meet the growing demand earned large profits. The refiner's margin by 1870 was $3.38 per hundred pounds (cwt), a very high level. This condition stimulated new investment of capital into the sugar refining industry. The frenzy of railroad building throughout the country added new markets for refined sugar, still largely produced in the Northeast. Theodore A. Havemeyer was quoted as saying that five-eighths of the sugar consumed in the country was refined in Brooklyn. Within five years of the end of the Civil War, the boom in the Eastern District had begun. Havemeyers & Elder was a growing giant. The only other important competition was from William Dick.

One will recall that Wintjen, Dick, and Schumacher left Manhattan in 1865 to buy a brick building at the foot of Division Avenue for their new refinery. Not only was this move eight years later than Havemeyer's, but it came right at the end of the Civil War, when consumer demand was light and materials hard to find. This most likely explains why they planned that their first refinery in Williamsburgh would be small. Undoubtedly they also did not have the capital then to build a larger one. It is interesting to note that when the refinery was moved to Williamsburgh, an office was opened at 109 Water Street in Manhattan. This was later moved to 87 Wall Street and finally to 110 Wall Street, being in the heart of the so-called sugar district of that famous street.

Not much is known about this Division Avenue refinery. Its capacity most likely was under 200,000 pounds per day. A map of 1868 shows another plot with the name Wintjen, Dick & Harms between South Second and South Third streets immediately next to the Havemeyers & Elder char house. This was probably a warehouse or distribution point operated in conjunction with the refinery on Division Avenue. It seems clear that as business expanded toward 1870-71, the Dick sugar house proved to be undersized. More space and capital were sorely needed. William Dick had begun acquiring parcels of land along North Seventh Street near the river in the mid-1860s, evidence that he knew when he left Manhattan that a much larger refinery, at least as large as the Havemeyers', would be needed very soon. In 1872 Dick found a new partner, Cord Meyer, another German who had immigrated from Hannover in 1823 and lived in Maspeth, Queens, just to the north of Williamsburgh. The firm of Dick & Meyer was formed. Meyer supplied substantial capital to the firm, but it was Dick who was the active managing partner. The Division Avenue sugar house was sold to Moller, Sierck & Company, a New Jersey firm already established in the business, and the building on South Second Street was sold to Havemeyers & Elder.

By 1873 a brand-new refinery had been built and opened by Dick & Meyer at the foot of North Seventh Street, west of Kent Avenue. It was the most modern in the industry and large by any standard, with a rated capacity of 900,000 pounds per day:

> The business of the firm, now Dick & Meyer, has made wonderful growth, the capital invested has reached $1,500,000 while the annual product of the refinery reaches 355,000 barrels or about 100,000,000 pounds of refined sugar. The management of this vast interest is almost wholly in the hands of Mr. Dick, a position for which he is especially well fitted by reason of his intelligence, business sagacity and capacity for work. (Stiles, 1884)

Dick must have been well known to Frederick C. Havemeyer Jr., who was sixteen years his senior, and sometime around 1870 Dick must have become acquainted with Mr. Havemeyer's youngest son, Henry Osborne, who had just become a partner of Havemeyers & Elder. William Dick and H. O. Havemeyer, twenty-four years Dick's junior, would have much to do with each other in the years ahead.

At about the time the newest Dick refinery entered the field, several other competitors were joining as well. Profit margins were large for modern plants, and the expansion of the nation westward foretold of limitless opportunities for sugar refiners. From 1869 to 1874 six new refineries, including Dick's, were built in that mile and a quarter of waterfront in the Eastern District. In addition,

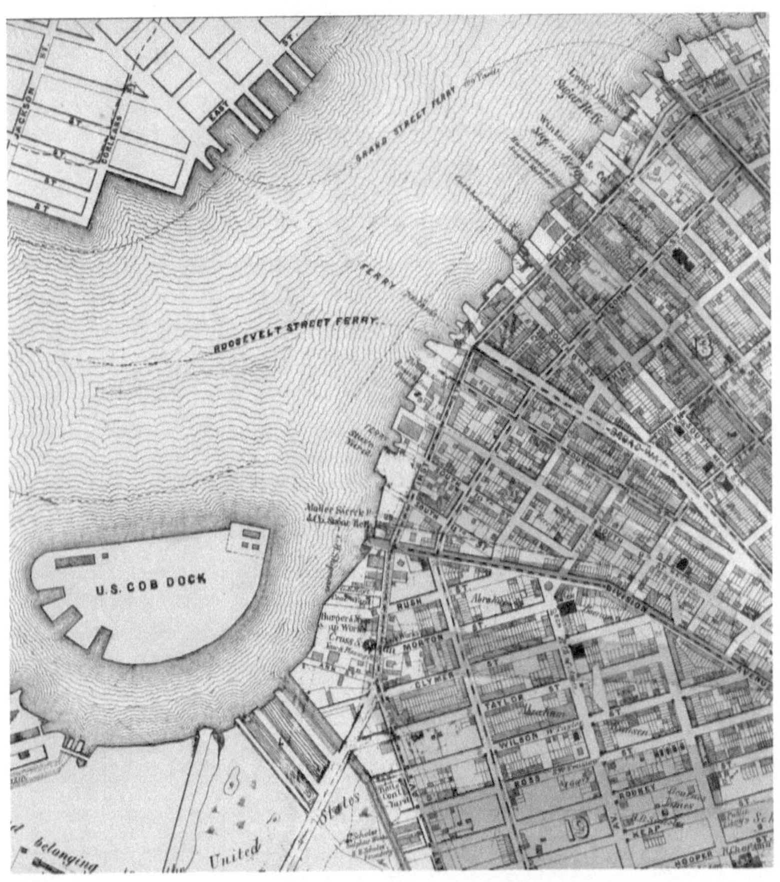

The 1869 map of Williamsburgh identifies four sugar refineries along the East River, from north to south, Long Island Sugar Refinery, Wintjen, Dick & Harms Sugar Refinery, Havemeyers & Elder Sugar Refinery, and Moller Sierck Sugar Refinery.

one was built in Greenpoint to the north and one in downtown Brooklyn to the south. Not all were large full-scale refineries. John Mollenhauer's molasses and syrup house, opened in 1869 and located on Rush Street, a block away from the Wallabout Creek entrance, lacked capital and was not a major competitor at that time. However, his business was well thought of:

> John Mollenhauer makes syrups his specialty, but also produces a considerable quantity of sugars, mostly, we believe by the centrifugal process [off-white turbinado sugar]. (Stiles, 1884)

This small specialty house could survive away from the riverfront because its products did not require the large space and equipment required in a full-scale refinery. Others to enter the business during this time were DeCastro & Donner, with two plants; the Brooklyn Sugar Refining Company; Moller, Sierck & Company; the Greenpoint Sugar Refining Company; and the Oxnard Brothers Refinery.

The major plants by 1874 in Brooklyn were:

- Havemeyers & Elder
- Greenpoint Sugar Refining Company
- DeCastro & Donner, with two refineries
- Brooklyn Sugar Refining Company
- Dick & Meyer

The smaller plants were:

- John Mollenhauer & Sons
- Moller, Sierck & Company
- Fulton Sugar Refining Company—Oxnard Brothers

A few brief words about some of those not already mentioned.

The Brooklyn Sugar Refining Company succeeded to the Long Island Sugar Refining Company between South First and South Second streets, west of Kent Avenue. Built in the early 1870s, it became a major factor in the industry and was operated by Claus

Doscher and Julius Stursberg—a competitor until 1887.* It was in the next block to the Havemeyers & Elder refinery complex.

DeCastro & Donner was established in 1870 when J. O. Donner promoted a refinery at the foot of South Ninth Street. It was engineered by John W. Booraem. It was the first to use cast-iron char filters. Business was so good that Donner promoted a second plant at the foot of North Second and North Third streets, also built by Booraem in 1873. To undertake this second plant, more capital was required, and DeCastro & Donner had to turn to the Havemeyers, who by 1874 ended up controlling both plants. As a side light, Booraem was also responsible for rebuilding the Havemeyers & Elder plant after the 1882 fire. The DeCastro & Donner plants were considered excellent ones, making particularly good soft or brown sugars.

The Greenpoint Sugar Refining Company, built around 1871, became the Havemeyer Sugar Refining Company in 1880. It was owned by the sons of William F. Havemeyer, mayor of New York. It was completely redesigned by Hector C. Havemeyer (1840-1889), who became president. Other officers were brothers Henry, James, and William F. Jr., and Treasurer John E. Searles Jr. It was a full-scale refinery with a 1,500,000-pound capacity and competed with those in the Williamsburgh area. As its first name implies, it was located on Commercial Street in Greenpoint. It suffered a disastrous fire in 1887 but was rebuilt afterwards. "This plant designed and built by Hector C. Havemeyer was very cleverly laid out and well run" (J. Henry Lienau).

The small Fulton Sugar Refining Company was acquired by the four Oxnard brothers, Robert, Benjamin, Henry T., and James G., in 1876. It was located in downtown Brooklyn inland from the East River at Washington Avenue and Sands Street. Its capacity

---

* Claus Doscher was born in Germany in 1830. He came to New York in 1848 and was employed in a grocery store. In 1876 he organized the Brooklyn Sugar Refining Company. He lived in the Eastern District in a house adjoining that of James H. Post on Ralph Street in 1900 at the time of the organization of the National Sugar Refining Company. (See Chapter 5.) He died in 1910.

was only 500 barrels per day. Although the Oxnards added some modern machinery, they never expanded the plant and it therefore was not competitive with the larger plants. It was operated intermittently until 1888. Its location at the plaza of the Brooklyn Bridge, which opened in 1883, severely restricted the operations of the refinery.

A reporter from the *Brooklyn Daily Eagle* described the waterfront scene in the 1880s:

> The most striking objects on the whole of Brooklyn's waterfront have yet to be mentioned. Just to the north of the Wallabout canal we come to the first of the series of sugar refineries, whose towering outlines on a foggy day, or in the last of the twilight, will suggest the lineaments of a Rhenish [sic] castle. We are here in the midst of the greatest sugar refining center in the world, where one establishment will sometimes in a single day convert 4,000,000 pounds of raw material into 12,000 barrels of refined sugar.

In this period of tremendous growth and new building of sugar plants, it is interesting to look at most of the names that have been mentioned: Havemeyer, Dick, Mollenhauer, Moller, Meyer, Booraem, Donner, Doscher. All are German. Although they did not all live in Williamsburgh—the Havemeyers never did—they and others were changing the Eastern District from a largely English and Irish community into a mostly German one.* William Dick, one will remember, had settled with his wife and young son John Henry in the Dutchtown area in 1857. By 1869 they had moved to a much more respectable and central area on South Ninth Street near Driggs Avenue, only two blocks from city center. Wil-

---

* Because such a large proportion of the sugar refinery employees could understand only German, notices from management were printed in both English and German. This practice was continued until near the end of the century.

liam Dick owned several houses on that block and became a major landowner in the area.

John Mollenhauer and his family did not move to Brooklyn until 1865, eleven years after his friend William Dick. Mollenhauer had gone from the grocery trade into the liquor importing business, which by 1860 was located at 256 Cherry Street, at the corner of Rutgers Street in Manhattan, just uptown from the Dick sugar house. He was so successful as a liquor wholesale dealer that he retired and went back to Hannover, Germany, to see his relatives there. Upon his return to America, he settled in Brooklyn on Marcy Avenue near Hart Street, a part of the Eastern District south of the Dutchtown area. He and his family remained there until 1875, when they moved to 156 Ross Street, only a few blocks from the Dicks. Four stories high, with an attractive cornice along the top, the house must have been a very satisfactory one for his family of five children. He remained there until his death.

During the last part of the 1870s and increasingly into the 1880s, competition amongst sugar refiners intensified. The vast new productive capacity brought about initially by high profit margins and growing demand resulted in a period of overproduction of refined sugar and sharply reduced margins. Annual per capita consumption held steady but profit margins went from $2.51 per cwt in 1876 to $0.712 in 1885, a clear indication of overproduction. Losses and ruin were in sight for all but the two or three largest, most efficient refiners. Long before 1887 it was realized that production must be limited and certain largely unsuccessful attempts were made. There were too many sellers in the business. Even as late as 1885 the firms of Havemeyers & Elder, DeCastro & Donner, the Brooklyn Sugar Refining Company, and Matthiesen & Weichers (in New Jersey) entered verbal agreements to curtail production. An attempt to halt production for a ten-day period failed. The situation looked bleak for the entire industry in the United States, as well as for the Brooklyn refiners.

It should be noted that the downward trend of profit margins during the period was broken only once, in the year 1882, when it actually rose somewhat. The reason for this unexpected reversal is clear, for on January 8, 1882, the Havemeyers & Elder plant burned down, and the largest producer of all was out of business. Fire was and always is a hazard in any manufacturing plant that uses steam, has machinery with moving parts, and heats ingredients to high temperatures. A sugar refinery is more hazardous than most because during the drying of the granulated sugar and the making of powdered sugar much dust is formed. This dust-filled air is particularly susceptible to spontaneous combustion under certain circumstances. (I personally witnessed a dust fire in the granulated house of the Long Island City Refinery in 1947.) It is not entirely unexpected, then, to read that three of the refineries mentioned so far burned down.

Immediately upon the destruction of the Havemeyers & Elder plant, the Havemeyer family determined to rebuild and to create the largest and most modern plant in the world. This they accomplished without any borrowed funds (a credit line with J. P. Morgan & Company was never used). While the rebuilding was underway, undoubtedly the three DeCastro & Donner plants that the Havemeyers controlled (one of these was in New Jersey) were operating at maximum capacity to protect the famous Havemeyers & Elder Eagle brand of sugar. When Theodore A. Havemeyer, John W. Booraem, and Ernest Gerbracht were finished rebuilding the burned-out refinery, the "jewel in the crown" was rated at 3,000,000 pounds per day with a cost of production far less than any other.* By 1883 Havemeyers & Elder was in such a dominant position in the industry that it could dictate terms to the others, and dictate is what it did. In 1883 with the huge new refinery in

---

* The new Havemeyers & Elder refinery was capable of producing a full assortment of soft or brown sugars as well as the "hard" or cube sugar, which was then known as patent cut loaf sugar and today is called Crystal Domino cubes and tablets. A fascinating description of the new Havemeyers & Elder refinery now covering the blocks between South Second and South Sixth Street from the *Brooklyn Daily Eagle* of July 30, 1883, is found in Appendix F.

operation, profit margins started to collapse again, and by 1885 they had fallen to $.712 per hundred pounds. Cutthroat competition was the order of the day. A solution to overproduction and price-cutting had to be found, and that solution, devised by Henry O. Havemeyer, now the leader of the firm, his attorney John E. Parsons, and John E. Searles of the Havemeyer Sugar Refining Company, was combination and consolidation—the creation in 1887 of the Sugar Refineries Company, usually called the Sugar Trust. A new era was about to begin for the whole United States sugar industry.

Above, the rebuilt Havemeyers & Elder refinery, c. 1895. *Below left*, Henry O. Havemeyer (1847-1907), c. 1885, and *right*, Theodore A. Havemeyer (1839-1897), 1893.

5

The Sugar Trust
and the Brooklyn Refineries
(1887–1907)

I will not discuss the entire development of the Sugar Trust in the United States but will limit my discussion as far as possible to the sugar refineries of the Eastern District and of lower Brooklyn. For most of them, consolidation and combination meant closure and demolishing.

It was most likely lawyer John E. Parsons who worked out the plan to establish the Sugar Refineries Company in 1887 at the direction of Henry O. and Theodore A. Havemeyer, the then seniors of Havemeyers & Elder. Parsons had been acquainted with the Havemeyers since 1873 and had previously represented them in sugar matters. The declared objectives of the plan were to keep sugar prices as low as was consistent with reasonable profit; to share technical information; to furnish protection against unlawful combinations of labor; and to promote the interests of the parties to the agreement. The design was patterned after the Standard Oil Trust of John D. Rockefeller, organized five years earlier. The independent sugar companies were "invited" to join into a combination for the purpose of controlling production and regulating prices. It was important that all or at least most of the major refiners join in. The companies were assigned a financial interest with a dollar value, based on a formula in which refinery capacity was the most important determining factor. Brand name was also important, and the Eagle brand of Havemeyers & Elder was the dominant one in the trade. "I would rather have the brand of Havemeyers & Elder than half of the other sugar refineries in the country," H. O. Havemeyer explained in 1899 before a U.S. Industrial Commission. A committee of five appraisers, headed by

Theodore A. Havemeyer, valued the property and inventory of the "invitee" company. Most of the independents wanted to join in for the economic advantages it would bring. Some held out for a while until they saw that the economic pressure brought by the Trust would cause bankruptcy if they failed to join. A few very small specialized refineries remained independent, and one refinery just happened to burn down after its owners refused to cooperate.

As well as controlling production, the Sugar Trust set refined sugar prices for all its companies. That crucial action was done by the mercantile committee, consisting in the beginning of Henry O. Havemeyer as chairman, John Jurgensen, Julius Stursberg, William Dick, John E. Searles, and John B. Thomas. From the start this group controlled all the key decisions that were made by the Trust and determined the level of profitability of every component part. For the most part, those few independents that followed the Trust-set price levels enjoyed benefits. So long as they did not increase their production they were left in peace. For the one or two that chose to fight the Trust, brutal economic warfare with severe price cutting was the result. In 1887 this was all legal activity, and indeed in 1895 the U.S. Supreme Court declared in the famous case *U. S. v. E. C. Knight* that sugar refining was in fact manufacturing, not commerce, and therefore could not be regulated by the federal government under the Sherman Anti-Trust Act of 1890. This ruling vindicated, at least in the eyes of H. O . Havemeyer, all of his actions on behalf of the partners in the Trust.

The Brooklyn refiners that entered the Sugar Refineries Company were as follows:

Refiner	Capital Stock
Havemeyers & Elder	$ 14,322,500
DeCastro & Donner	2,677,500
Havemeyer Sugar Refining Co.	4,675,000
Brooklyn Sugar Refining Co.	3,612,500

Dick & Meyer	2,550,000
Moller, Sierck & Company	912,500
Oxnard Brothers	637,500

The only refinery that did not join was John Mollenhauer's molasses house on Rush Street. His independence was accepted by the Trust because at that time his plant's output was only molasses and syrups and could in no way threaten the balance and control of refined sugar price levels.

The original trustees were eleven men divided into three classes:

(1) *For seven years*: Henry O. Havemeyer; F. O. Matthiessen (New Jersey refiner); John E. Searles (Havemeyer Sugar Refining Company); Julius A. Stursberg (Brooklyn Sugar Refining Company)

(2) *For five years*: Theodore A. Havemeyer (named the president); Joseph B. Thomas (Boston refiner); Hector C. Havemeyer, cousin of H. O. Havemeyer (Havemeyer Sugar Refining Company); John Jurgensen (New Jersey refiner) (3) *For three years*: Charles H. Senff (Havemeyers & Elder refiner); William Dick (Dick & Meyer); Charles O. Foster (Boston refiner)

Clearly, Havemeyers & Elder with three seats, the friendly cousin Hector, and John E. Searles controlled the board. Although Theodore was nominally president, Henry O. Havemeyer was the central figure because of his experience and proven ability in the commercial end of the business where he had always concentrated. He was generally considered the greatest sugar merchant of his era. It is hard to determine what role William Dick played, except to say that it must have been a cooperative one. He freely entered the Trust, and received, on behalf of himself and his partner, Cord Meyer, $2,550,000 of stock for their refinery on North Seventh Street. When the Trust reorganized as the American Sugar Refining Company in 1891, he became a director and remained so until 1898. However, his principal activities had shifted after 1887 to banking and other philanthropic interests. Because by now Dick was a senior citizen and leading figure in Brooklyn, it was probably important to the Havemeyers to have him involved with the Sugar Trust, and besides, he owned a large amount of American Sugar preferred and common stock. It was also known that he was very close to the Mollenhauers,* and in 1891 that was particularly important, as they were then considering a major expansion of their business.

The first important action taken by the Sugar Trust was to decrease the cost of production by increasing the efficiency of its plants; and to determine which were the most efficient, a competition among them was conducted. For sixty days they would run at full capacity as a test. At the end, those with the lowest costs would survive; the others would be closed—survival of the fittest in manufacturing. Those with the larger capacities had a tremendous advantage in the race, as high volume of production is the key to low unit costs. When it was over, just five refineries had survived the test, and only one in Brooklyn—the Havemeyers & Elder giant.

The earlier of the two DeCastro & Donner plants on South Ninth Street was dismantled, and the property became the site of the Brooklyn Distilling Company, a predecessor of the F. & M. Schaefer Brewery there. The North Second/North Third Street plant was kept in reserve and used only as a warehouse until 1914, when the site was used to build the new Austin-Nichols building.

The Greenpoint refinery of the Havemeyer Sugar Refining Company suffered a disastrous fire in June 1887. The decision was taken to rebuild it and to use it as a standby, operating only in the summer and other periods of peak demand. It was finally dismantled in 1906 and much of its equipment moved to Chalmette, Louisiana, where the American Sugar Refining Company's new refinery was built.

---

* Dick's son John Henry had married Mollenhauer's daughter Julia, and Mollenhauer's son J. Adolph had married Dick's daughter Anna.

The Brooklyn Sugar Refinery Company's South First/South Second Street plant right next to the Havemeyers & Elder plant was consolidated into it and the two plants were operated as a unit.

The Dick & Meyer refinery was operating, at least part-time, until September 7, 1889, when it too was destroyed by fire. It was not rebuilt.

The smaller Moller, Sierck and Company and Oxnard Brothers plants were dismantled in 1888. As mentioned previously, Mollenhauer's molasses house continued to run as an independent until 1891.

Almost overnight there existed a very different scene in the Eastern District. By 1891 there was just one huge sugar refinery in operation; it extended from South First to South Sixth streets—five waterfront blocks, with several inland parcels as well. In that year, the American Sugar Refining Company was organized, incorporated in the State of New Jersey, and Henry O. Havemeyer became its first president. Because of complicated legal difficulties in the State of New York, the Sugar Refineries Company was forced to dissolve, and its assets were turned over to the newly founded concern. There were seven directors: Henry O. Havemeyer, president; Theodore A. Havemeyer; John E. Searles; William Dick; John B. Thomas; F. O. Matthiessen; and George C. Magoun. Except for Magoun, these were all familiar names.[*] The capital of the company was $25 million of preferred stock and $25 million of common stock, making it one of the very largest companies in the United States. H. O. Havemeyer said to the press at the time: "Well, from being illegal as we were, we are now legal as we are; change enough, isn't it?" Over the next fifteen years or so the American Sugar Refining Company steadily grew, first by gaining control over all the Philadelphia refineries, and then over most of the sugar production, refining and beet, in the entire United States. By 1907, the year of H. O. Havemeyer's death, it

---

[*]   Hector C. Havemeyer had died in 1889. Charles H. Senff and the lawyer John E. Parsons would become directors a few years later. See Appendix D.

The Mollenhauer Sugar Refinery was built by John Mollenhauer and his sons. *Above*, an illustration of the refinery c. 1898 and, *below*, a photograph, c. 1904.

was said to control 98 percent of the refined sugar sold in the country—a complete monopoly.

However, in the Eastern District of Brooklyn, the Havemeyers & Elder refinery was not the sole refinery for long, for by the end of 1891, because of the McKinley Tariff,* the Mollenhauers opened a new refinery to compete against the Sugar Trust, a courageous—some might have said foolhardy—decision to make. In John Mollenhauer's obituary notice in the *New York Times* on January 1, 1905, he was described thusly:

> The refiner who fought the Sugar Trust is dead ...
> He rejected all overtures from the Trust and
> fought it consistently until 1900, when his busi-
> ness ... interests were combined in the National
> Sugar Refining Company.

The Mollenhauer company was very much a family affair. John, aged sixty-five, was the president, and each of his four sons was an officer: Adolph, vice president and general manager; Frederick, secretary and treasurer; Henry, superintendent; William, assistant secretary and treasurer. Producing a complete line of sugars with a capacity of 1,200,000 pounds per day, the refinery was located on the waterfront between the foot of Division Avenue and the foot of South Eleventh Street just a block away from their "old" molasses house, and interestingly, just across the street from the now demolished Wintjen & Dick sugar house of 1865. The map of

---

* In 1890 two significant pieces of legislation were passed by the Congress and signed by President Benjamin Harrison. The first was the Sherman Anti-Trust Act, referred to earlier; the second was the McKinley Tariff. This latter bill was a high tariff act that sought not only to protect established industry but also to foster new industry in the U.S. by prohibitory duties on many foreign imports. However, it put foreign raw sugar on the "free of duty" list and compensated Louisiana cane growers and the few Western beet farmers with a bounty of two cents a pound. The McKinley Tariff thus dramatically lowered the cost of raw sugar to U.S. refiners, encouraged Cuban raw sugar production, and discouraged the import of foreign molasses. As a result, sugar refining was made much more profitable, but the so-called molasses houses were put out of business.

1887 shows the Mollenhauers as owning a storage yard on the site. It is likely therefore that the expansion had been contemplated for some time. The Mollenhauers, however, did not sell their sugar themselves. They contracted with the firm of B. H. Howell Sons & Company,* sugar brokers and merchants, to sell all of their output. That firm was directed at the time by James Howell Post (1859-1938).

In spite of the obituary notice cited above, the Mollenhauers did not intend to compete against the Sugar Trust at all, using the strict sense of that word. They intended to work in harmony with and to follow the prices set by the Trust; by doing so, to attain the benefits of that umbrella and to enjoy the economic climate provided by the McKinley Tariff. Others had done this successfully. Revere in Boston was an example. At the time Mollenhauer's refinery was built, the Sugar Trust had its hands full fighting Spreckels in Philadelphia and acquiring the Franklin and E. C. Knight refineries in that city—all much larger plants and therefore more important factors in the Trust's goals to control production and set prices. Also, the B. H. Howell Sons firm was known to be "friendly" to the Trust and did not try to upset established sugar prices. In fact, Charles H. Senff of the Sugar Trust bought 30 percent of the Mollenhauer stock to help finance the new refinery, and later in March 1893 he sold this stock to the Sugar Trust, which then became a Mollenhauer "partner." In any event, the refinery was built and operated until 1901, just nine years.

During the decade of the 1890s three other new refineries were built in New York harbor, although only one was in Brooklyn. First, in 1893 the National Refinery was built in Yonkers by George R.

---

* Benjamin Huntting Howell was born in 1811 in Bellport, Long Island. He moved to New York and established a wholesale grocery business in 1832. In 1861 he admitted his son Thomas as a partner, and the firm B. H. Howell & Son began to trade in sugar and molasses. In the 1870s other partners were added as the firm grew in size and prosperity. It was located at 91 Wall Street and later at 109 Wall Street. B. H. Howell lived for most of his life in the Eastern District and died in 1900 at his home at 96 South Ninth Street, a block away from the Dicks.

Bunker, his brother Albert, and the Tooker family; it had a capacity similar to that of the Mollenhauer plant.* Its output was turned over for sale to B. H. Howell Sons, whose partners were stockholders in the company as well. "B. H. Howell Sons & Co. became commission merchants for the Mollenhauer and National refineries and refused to lose money by competing with the Trust" (*U.S. Industrial Commission Reports*).

Second, Claus Doscher and his sons,** who had taken their Brooklyn refinery into the Trust in 1887, decided to build a new one in Long Island City on the Queens side of Newtown Creek, just across from the Greenpoint refinery (formerly Havemeyer Sugar Refining Company). It opened in November 1898 with a somewhat larger capacity than Mollenhauer's and National-Yonkers. In the beginning, competition between Doscher and the Trust was vigorous, but soon Henry O. Havemeyer had found a way to manage that problem as well. "Doscher always believed that his refinery was able to refine as cheaply as any other, but he was never able to realize any profit except in trading in a rising market" (*U.S. Industrial Commission Reports*). George R. Bunker was later quoted as saying that Doscher, being the newest in the field, was always cutting prices to get business and thereby upsetting the market.

Third, John Arbuckle, the coffee merchant, entered the sugar refining business to counter the entry of the Trust in the coffee

---

* George R. Bunker (1845-1927), a contemporary of H. O. Havemeyer, was general manager at the Delaware Sugar Refining Company, a molasses house, from 1869 until 1892, when it was purchased by the American Sugar Refining Company and merged into the Spreckels Refinery next door. The Delaware Sugar Refining Company was started by Bunker's uncle, John Wilson, and by B. H. Howell Sons & Company. Other shareholders were Mrs. Crabb, Bunker, James H. Post from Brooklyn, and J. Vaughn Merrick from Philadelphia. In 1892 Bunker moved to Yonkers to build the new refinery there. He served as a director of the National Sugar Refining Company from 1900 to 1921. He was also a founder and director of the Cuban American Sugar Company with Post.

** Henry, Charles, and John Doscher. Other owners were Julius Stursberg and Caroline Weidmann for Paul Weidmann, deceased. (See Chapter 7.)

business. His refinery, begun in 1896 and opened in August 1898, was located on the waterfront at the foot of Jay and Pearl streets in what is called downtown Brooklyn, just north of the future Manhattan Bridge. The refinery's capacity was rated at 1,500,000 pounds. It was managed by J. F. Stillman and produced "very handsome soft sugars, much better than that at Havemeyers & Elder" (J. H. Lienau). The building of the Arbuckle refinery started the famous Havemeyer-Arbuckle war, waged brutally and vigorously for three years. No holds were barred in the battle. It continued until early in 1901, when H. O. Havemeyer and John Arbuckle settled and Arbuckle agreed to limit his production. Arbuckle's was the last refinery to be built in Brooklyn until the 1930s. It continued to operate until the end of 1940.

In 1900, as has been seen, Claus Doscher was causing much trouble for the Sugar Trust.* Henry O. Havemeyer decided the time had come to "manage" that problem and proceeded to combine the Mollenhauer, the Yonkers, and the Doscher refineries into the National Sugar Refining Company of New Jersey, incorporated on May 31, 1900, with a capital of $10,000,000 of preferred stock and $10,000,000 of common stock. It was agreed that B. H. Howell Sons should be the exclusive agent for the new company's sugar, and James Howell Post was made president. Howell and Post would have control over the purchase of raw sugar, the sale of refined sugar, and the financing of the company. The company directors would control only the operations at the refineries. Furthermore, the Mollenhauer plant, being the least efficient, would be kept on standby, and only the Yonkers and Long Island City ones would continue to run on a regular basis.

To create this combination, H. O. Havemeyer and James H. Post planned a complicated series of financial transactions which resulted in the Mollenhauer stockholders, the Bunker-Tookers in-

---

* The National-Yonkers refinery had been closed for seventeen months due to unprofitable market conditions; the Mollenhauer refinery had been closed for six months.

Havemeyer—"Come John, it's your move."

Above, a cartoon depicting the Havemeyer and Arbuckle battle over sugar prices and markets, April 12, 1900. *Below*, a cartoon depicting H. O. Havemeyer, creator of the Sugar Trust, endorsing the tariff bill, c. 1900.

MR. HAVEMEYER PAINTS A PICTURE.

terests, and the Doscher stockholders owning slightly less than half of the new company's outstanding preferred shares, which were to pay a 6 percent dividend. The rest of the outstanding preferred shares (slightly more than a half) were owned by the American Sugar Refining Company, most having been purchased for cash. In return for providing his credit and his "cooperation" in making the combination possible, H.O. Havemeyer personally received all the common shares.* He immediately assigned 5 percent of them to Post, the new president of the company, and arranged as well that they all be registered in Post's name. They were, however, voted in accord with Havemeyer's instructions. Post claimed later in 1911 that it was necessary to accede to this demand in order to organize the new company at all. By the time of Havemeyer's death in 1907 he owned only 17 percent of the common shares, having given 76 percent of them to his children in trust and having sold 1 percent to F. D. Mollenhauer, National's treasurer, and 1 percent to J. H. Dick, a National director.

The question of whether H.O. Havemeyer exercised control over the National after 1900 is open to differing interpretations. The fact remains, he could have if he had wanted to. He owned the common stock. The Sugar Trust of which he was the head owned more than half the preferred stock, and in addition had lent the new company over $2,000,000. Furthermore, he did suggest to Post the names of three directors from the Sugar Trust who were elected National directors in December 1905.** However, both Post and Havemeyer's son Horace, in 1911 after Havemeyer's death, denied under oath that he did in fact exercise any control

---

* Havemeyer's son Horace testified in 1911 that the personal credit of his father and mother was required in order that Post be able to borrow the funds to pay for the preferred stock of National that he was almost immediately to resell to the American—i.e., $4,250,000 at par.

** John Mayer (Theodore A. Havemeyer's son-in-law), Arthur Donner and George H. Frazier. They remained National Sugar directors until January 1910. See Appendix E.

at all.* It is likely that Post, B. H. Howell Sons, and National's board knew what they were supposed to do without any instructions—i.e., act in harmony with the Sugar Trust goals and reap the benefits thereof. B. H. Howell received special allowances on sugar sold, and the preferred and common shareholders prospered when the Sugar Trust did. In 1903, a 10 percent dividend was paid on National common stock, the preferred paying its regular 6 percent. In 1904 a 15 percent dividend was paid. Margins of profit from 1901 to 1907 were from 90¢ to $1.00 per hundred pounds higher than for the three previous years.

The relationship between H. O. Havemeyer and James H. Post should be examined more closely. Post, twelve years younger than Havemeyer, had started as an office boy at B. H. Howell Sons & Company in 1874, in the midst of the great expansion of refineries in Brooklyn where he lived. He became a partner of the firm in 1887, the year the Sugar Trust was formed. Certainly by then he had become acquainted with Havemeyer. As a senior partner in the 1890s, selling sugar for the Mollenhauers and for the Yonkers refinery, he must have been carefully watched by Havemeyer, and a relationship of trust developed. In 1898 Post was elected to the board of directors of the National City Bank of New York, where he became a banking colleague with his fellow director H. O. Havemeyer. Therefore when the National Sugar Refining Company was formed in 1900 it was very natural that Post should be chosen president, most likely by Havemeyer. Furthermore, Havemeyer did not want the Mollenhauer sons or George Bunker or Claus Doscher in charge. The exclusive contract with B. H. Howell Sons & Company would foreclose that possibility. This relationship of trust between Havemeyer and Post was also confirmed in their involvement with the Cuban American Sugar Company. This company, formed in 1906 to control several Cuban

---

* Testimony during hearings of U.S. House of Representatives, Special Committee on Investigation of the American Sugar Refining Company and others, 1911-1912. Rep. Hardwick, Chairman.

raw sugar properties, used B. H. Howell as its sole commercial agent to sell its sugars. Post was its treasurer and a director as well. H.O. Havemeyer was a major investor in Cuban American Sugar, and his stock was held in Post's name. In public testimony after Havemeyer's death, Post declared: "I welcome the opportunity to go on record in regard to my high opinion of Mr. Havemeyer's ability and honor."*

The Mollenhauer family all became large National preferred shareholders as a result of the reorganization. Although their refinery was closed in 1901, it was retained by National for some years as a standby and was used to warehouse sugar. The property was subsequently sold to their neighbor, the Brooklyn Distilling Company. The Mollenhauer sons took an active interest in the National. Fred was a director, vice president, and treasurer from the start until his death in 1914. He was succeeded on the board by his brother Adolph, who served until his death in 1926. The youngest brother, Henry, was a director from 1900 until his death in 1931 and served as assistant treasurer and then treasurer after Fred died. The family retained its interest into the 1940s.

The Dick family also became stockholders of National Sugar. When the new Mollenhauer refinery was built in 1891, John Henry Dick made a large investment in the new enterprise of his wife's family in spite of the fact that his father was still a director of the Sugar Trust at the time. In fact, the Trust itself had owned 30 percent of the Mollenhauer stock since 1893. Being intermarried two ways, the Mollenhauers and Dicks shared common interests in sugar, particularly National. John Henry Dick became a National director in 1901, succeeding Claus Doscher. In addition to Post, the Mollenhauers and J. H. Dick, early directors included George R. Bunker and Nathaniel Tooker representing the Yonkers

---

* Testimony during hearings of U.S. House of Representatives, Special Committee on Investigation of the American Sugar Refining Company and others, 1911-1912. Rep. Hardwick, Chairman.

interests and Thomas A. Howell and Fred H. Howell of B. H. Howell Sons (see Appendix E).

What was the relationship between H. O. Havemeyer and William Dick? Dick, the elder by twenty-four years, must have been something of the elder statesman. Although he retired from the management of a sugar business in 1887, he was an active investor in sugar, banking, and real estate until the end of his life, in 1912. He often invested in the same sugar interests as Havemeyer: the American Sugar Refining Company, of course (he received a large amount of that stock for his refinery), but also Cuban American Sugar and Guantanamo Sugar. He remained a director of the Sugar Trust until 1898, when he retired at the age of seventy-five.* After his retirement he was elected an advisory member of the Mercantile Committee and paid a modest salary. Clearly the two men were close, and one suspects that Havemeyer had considerable respect for the old gentleman who had started with nothing at all.

The period of industry domination by the Sugar Trust was ending by the close of 1907. Havemeyer had died on December 4, 1907; Mollenhauer, three years earlier. Dick was to live in retirement for five years more. The waterfront in Brooklyn looked quite different in the Eastern District. On the northwest point of Newtown Creek the Long Island City refinery of the National Sugar Refining Company with a rated capacity now of 2,000,000 pounds per day operated under the management of J. Henry Lienau and would continue to expand its output. It closed and was dismantled in 1964. Along the Greenpoint shore were the shipbuilders, the lumberyards, and the iron foundries. Arriving in the 1860s they dominated the northern part of the Eastern District. That famous ironclad the Monitor was launched in 1862 from the Continental Iron Works in Greenpoint. She destroyed the Merrimac that year

---

* Dick also held the title of second vice president from 1892 to 1898. It is unlikely, however, that he was involved in the daily management of the Trust.

off Cape Hatteras and began an irreversible trend toward iron-hulled ships.

South of Newtown Creek, where all the sugar refineries had been located in the 1870s and 1880s, there was operating now only the huge Havemeyers & Elder plant, with a rated capacity at this time of 5,000,000 pounds per day. It extended from Grand Street south to South Fifth Street—four blocks, its southernmost block having been sold to the City of Brooklyn for the building of the Williamsburgh Bridge, which was completed in 1903. To the south of the bridge was a large ferry terminal, the Brooklyn Distillery Company, and the dormant Mollenhauer refinery.

Lastly, to the south of Wallabout Bay was the sugar refinery of the Arbuckle Brothers mentioned earlier. It had a rated capacity now of 2,500,000 pounds per day and continued in production until 1940, when it too was dismantled.

An epilogue to this chapter should include the events of 1911 concerning the National Sugar Refining Company. The owner-ship of that company was as follows at the beginning of that year: Almost half of the preferred stock was in the hands of the Mol-lenhauers, Dicks, Bunkers, Tookers, Doschers, and McCahans;* the other half was owned by the American Sugar Refining Com-pany; 95,000 of the 100,000 shares of the common stock were owned by the heirs of the late H. O. Havemeyer, although still in the nominee of James H. Post, National's president. H. O. Have-meyer's only son, Horace, twenty-four years old, had resigned in December 1910 as a director of the American, in which post he had served since his father's death three years before. In January he advised Post and the National directors that he wished to be

---

* The McCahan molasses house in Philadelphia was converted into a sugar refinery in 1892, because of the McKinley Tariff, at the same time as the Mollenhauers converted theirs in New York (see above). In June 1900 the McCahan family sold a one-quarter interest in their refinery to the National Sugar Refining Company within a week after the latter was organized in return for $1,470,000 National preferred stock.

William Dick, merchant and banker of Williamsburgh.

elected a director and vice-president of National, that he wished the exclusive selling contract with B. H. Howell Sons ended, and that he himself would undertake the responsibility of selling sugar for the company. Finally, he advised Post to have the 95,000 shares transferred from Post's name to his, as his family's sole male heir. He intended to take over control of the company by virtue of ownership of this common stock and to manage it himself in direct competition with the American, in which company he no longer had any financial interest. With over five years experience by then of selling sugar for the Sugar Trust, he was surely qualified to undertake doing so for National. His qualifications were never questioned. But the American did not want competition, at least not this kind, even after H. O. Havemeyer's death, and they objected. Because of this objection, Post refused to transfer the common shares to Horace Havemeyer as requested. Then the other preferred shareholders, led by the Tookers on behalf of the Mollenhauers, Dicks, et al., instituted an action in court at the instigation of the American to invalidate all the common shares on the ground that they were issued to H. O. Havemeyer in 1900 without compensation. All of this occurred in January and February of 1911. As the legal action was getting under way and making headlines in the daily papers, on February 28 Horace Havemeyer was married to Doris Dick, granddaughter of William Dick and John Mollenhauer, and thus an heiress of two of the families that were suing her husband.

The suit went on during all of 1911. In July 1912 the court finally found for the plaintiff and declared the National common stock invalid. Havemeyer did not choose to appeal. As a result of this decision the Havemeyer family had no connection with the National at all after 1912. Their investment had been invalidated. The preferred stockholders became the common stockholders, which meant, ironically, that the American now owned over half the common stock and clearly could control the company. James H. Post remained president until 1935 and the Mollenhauer and Dick families, as discussed earlier, continued their active roles. William K. Dick, grandson of William Dick and John Mollenhauer, became a director in 1923 and served until his death in 1953. He was also a vice president, chairman of the executive committee, and chairman of the board successively. The American Sugar Refining Company reduced its interest in National from 50 percent to 25 percent following 1912. It was not until 1944, however, that at long last they found a buyer for that remaining 25 percent, and that buyer was none other than Horace Havemeyer.

The Manufacturers National Bank, with which William Dick was primarily associated, circa 1905. The building minus the cupola stands today.

6

Banking in Williamsburgh
(1853–1912)

The year 1853 saw the first insurance company and the first banks opened in Williamsburgh. This coincided with the formal designation of Williamsburgh as a city and the start of its conversion to a large manufacturing and industrial area, at least along the waterfront. These financial institutions were first located on or just off Kent Avenue, which might have been called the city center of the 1850s.

The first bank to open was the Williamsburgh Savings Bank. Incorporated in 1851, it actually opened for business in 1853 and was located on South Third Street at the Bedford Avenue corner. Its first president was Samuel Meeker, and its first trustees were among the 1847 list of solid men of Williamsburgh. Noah Waterbury, his son James, and William Wall, the second mayor, headed the list. Wall succeeded Meeker as president after his term as mayor. This savings bank began as the bank for the leading citizens of the city and was to continue as the establishment bank. In 1875 it moved to its present site on Broadway at Driggs Avenue, where a handsome building with a dome roof was built. By 1925 it was the largest savings bank in Brooklyn.

The first commercial bank, the Williamsburgh City Bank, opened in 1853 as well. Its first president was Noah Waterbury.* These banks were very small when they opened, and it was not at all unusual for Waterbury to be a trustee of one and president of another. Banking was not a full-time occupation then, and conflicts of interest were not of great concern. The first insurance

---

* As mentioned in Chapter 3, Noah Waterbury was Williamsburgh's earliest merchant, with his distillery at South Second Street and his several "ropewalks."

company, the Williamsburgh City Fire Insurance Company, also opened that year. Its first president was Edmund Driggs, and men such as Wall, Waterbury, and Berry were trustees. Leading citizens performed many tasks, both economic and political, in that era.

The next bank to open also in 1853 was the Mechanics Bank of Williamsburgh. It was located on the ground floor of the same building as the Williamsburgh City Fire Insurance Company—16 Grand Street, just off Kent Avenue. The Mechanics Bank continued there until 1865, when it moved to Manhattan. Later, experiencing difficulties, it went into a reorganization and became the Manufacturers National Bank in 1873, relocating back in Williamsburgh and occupying a new building on the southwest corner of Broadway and Berry Street—84 Broadway. William Dick was associated with this bank for almost forty years as a director and large shareholder. He served as a vice-president until 1903, when at age eighty he became the president, retiring in 1907 from that office. His son was a vice-president as well. John Mollenhauer and Lur Wintjen were directors with him. The bank merged on August 1, 1914 (after Dick and Mollenhauer had died), with the Citizens Trust Company. A year later the word Citizens was dropped and the bank became the Manufacturers Trust Company. By this time the Mollenhauer sons had joined the board and William K. Dick had replaced his grandfather. The Manufacturers Trust Company subsequently expanded into Manhattan again, to merge with the Hanover Bank, becoming the Manufacturers Hanover Bank. A small branch of this giant bank continues to occupy the ground floor of 84 Broadway in Williamsburgh today.

In addition to the Manufacturers National Bank, William Dick was closely involved with the German Savings Bank. This bank was opened in 1866 in the area called Dutchtown at 84 Montrose Avenue. It was "intended to accommodate Germans as a class, who were noted for their thrifty habits."* This was very near where Dick and his family first lived in Williamsburgh—the German

---

*   Eugene L. Armbruster, *Brooklyn's Eastern District.*

section—and it is likely that his involvement with it predates his involvement with the Manufacturers National Bank. In 1875 the German Savings Bank moved to Broadway and Boerum Street, some three blocks away. While it was located here, Dick became its third president for a time. He later served as vice-president.

> When the prospects of the German Savings Bank were dark, an appeal was made to [Dick] to lend his assistance and assume its management. Accepting the Presidency he restored credit and confidence, placed the institution on a firm footing, and at the end of the second year left it prosperous, resigning his office only on account of the fast increasing demands of his own business.*

Although it is not possible to date exactly the time of the bank's financial difficulties, it is likely that it was in the period of 1873 to 1876, when the stock market crash and the depression put many banks throughout the United States in bankruptcy. It was at this time as well that the Manufacturers National reorganized and returned to Williamsburgh. Dick remained a trustee of the German Savings Bank until his retirement. The bank's name was changed in 1918 to the Lincoln Savings Bank because of the strong anti-German prejudice in the United States during World War I.

The third bank Dick was associated with in his post-sugar-refining period was the Nassau Trust Company. Opened in 1888, it was located on Broadway and Bedford Avenue, on the southwest corner, just one block east of the Manufacturers National. William Dick was listed as a vice-president and trustee. James H. Post was a trustee as well.

Lastly, in 1884, in downtown Brooklyn, the Long Island Loan & Trust Company opened for business. Among its charter trustees were three familiar names: William Dick, Theodore A. Havemeyer (brother of Henry O.), and Lowell M. Palmer (see Chapter 7). A

---

* L. P. Brockett, "Banking of Williamsburgh," in Henry Reed Stiles, ed., *The History of Kings County.*

The German Savings Bank of Brooklyn. William Dick saved this bank from financial ruin. Depicted here c. 1905, the building no longer remains.

branch was also established on Broadway and Berry Street. This trust company was merged into the Brooklyn Trust Company in 1913.

William Dick, the German immigrant, successful sugar refiner, and now the senior citizen banker of Williamsburgh, did not ever forget where his roots lay. As the reader will see later, he involved himself in all aspects of the Brooklyn German-American community and its needs.

Jumping back in time to 1864, the Dime Savings Bank of Williamsburgh opened that year on the southwest corner of Broadway and Kent Avenue near the waterfront. "It was founded to serve particularly those of moderate means and to encourage them in the act of saving."* By 1873 and the beginning of the waterfront industrial boom, it built its own building on the southwest corner of Broadway and Wythe Avenue—52 Broadway—just one block further inland and one block away from the Manufacturers National Bank. The Dime Savings Bank of Williamsburgh was the bank with which John Mollenhauer was most closely involved. He was a trustee for eighteen years prior to his death, and served as president from 1898 to 1904. His youngest son Henry was a trustee as well, from 1900 to 1914. The name of the sugar refiner, Claus Doscher, was also found on its board. The Dime grew rapidly from those early beginnings. By 1908 the Dime had made its last move eastward to 209 Havemeyer Street at the corner of South Fifth Street, where it is today.

By 1875 the principal banks were all lined up on Broadway going inland from the river to Driggs Avenue. That had become the new center city, still close to the industrial waterfront, but conveniently somewhat away and headed inland toward Dutchtown.

The other Mollenhauer banking connection was not in Williamsburgh at all. John's son, J. Adolph, was for many years prior to his death in 1926 a trustee of the Brooklyn Trust Company. This old established bank (opened in 1866) was among many in down-

---

* *Dime Savings Bank of Williamsburgh 50th Anniversary 1864-1914.*

Above, the Dime Savings Bank of Williamsburgh. John Mollenhauer was a director of this bank, shown here at its new location on Havemeyer Street at the corner of South Fifth Street in 1908. It stands there today. *Below*, the Williamsburgh Bridge Plaza. The bridge has just been opened. The domed building is the Williamsburgh Savings Bank, designed by George B. Post and standing there today.

town Brooklyn. It was the trustee for the estates of J. Adolph and his wife, Anna Dick Mollenhauer, who died in 1935. Its president for a time was Edwin P. Maynard, the father of Henry F. Mollenhauer's son-in-law. In 1950 it was merged into the Manufacturers Trust Company of New York.

What is perhaps most striking when one looks at banking in Williamsburgh during this sixty-year period from 1853 to 1912 is first the great number of small banks that sprang up to serve the growing industrial area (by no means all have been discussed), and second, the several connections and close involvement of William Dick and John Mollenhauer in this field of endeavor. Although Dick and Mollenhauer both remained involved in different ways in sugar and molasses refining, at the same time they also moved easily into banking. The picture emerges of respected elders on the Williamsburgh scene, never denying their strong German heritage in spite of pressures to do so. They both remained in their Williamsburgh homes to their deaths at advanced ages (eighty-nine and seventy-seven respectively).

The Brooklyn Cooperage Company plant, circa 1911, on the East River between North 6th and North 7th streets.

7

Real Estate, Cooperage and Transportation (1870-1912)

Sugar refining in the modern era required large amounts of space on which to locate the several buildings housing this capital-intensive, high-volume process. Auxiliary to the main process but essential to it was the need for nearby transportation facilities, both rail and horse-drawn wagons, and a large supply of barrels in which the refined sugar could be shipped. Rail transportation and cooperage grew in size and importance as the refineries themselves grew, requiring still more land. Rail transportation in Brooklyn required waterfront land. Cooperage could be located inland provided it could be served by a rail depot where the wooden staves from the West could be unloaded. Coal for fuel was also brought from the West by rail directly to the refinery coal yard. Thus a very good freight business was created: sugar in barrels going west, and coal and staves going east. In the early 1870s all the seven main trunk line railroads competed for this business had established depots in the Eastern District. Because of the particular geography of New York harbor, a rail depot in the Eastern District was connected to the main track on the New Jersey shore by a "float"—a barge with rails on it—pulled by a tug back and forth across the harbor and connected at the shore line by a float bridge. Each of the trunk line railroads had tugs, floats, and float bridges at their Jersey terminals, but at the Eastern District end they had a problem. There was not enough available space on the waterfront for seven separate float bridges, rail yards, and unloading stations. In fact at each refinery there was only one float bridge, and it was owned by the refinery, not by the railroad. The railroads also found that the little empty waterfront land just happened to be in the area of North Fourth to North Tenth streets and with a single exception it was all owned by Havemeyers & Elder.

Most likely in the late 1860s, but certainly by 1870, the Havemeyers & Elder firm began acquiring waterfront real estate. This occurred long before the Sugar Trust was established, when the other refiners were entirely independent. Seeing the value of this property before the others, Havemeyers & Elder assembled over a period of time much of the vacant waterfront north of Grand Street to North Tenth Street. They also acquired several inland blocks between Kent Avenue and Wythe Avenue and between Wythe Avenue and Berry Street. This was to give the firm control of the area and the cooperage and transportation facilities that were needed to service *all* of the refineries. It was a forerunner, if you will, of the formation of the Trust.

The individual most responsible for the land acquisition, cooperage, and transportation activities in this area was a young man named Lowell M. Palmer (1845-1915). Palmer, a nephew of the sugar engineer John W. Booraem, was born in Ohio. He enlisted in the Northern army and fought in the Civil War. Upon its conclusion, he moved to Brooklyn, where he settled in the Eastern District and began a career in the development of that waterfront area. He was an ambitious man and entrepreneurial by nature. However, he lacked capital himself. It is not known just when he came to the attention of Havemeyers & Elder, but it is known that he established Palmer's Dock at the foot of North Fifth and North Sixth Street by 1870, and leased to the Erie Railroad a terminus or float bridge there. From 1873 on, he cast his lot with the Havemeyers and their capital. The relationship lasted thirty-three years. Palmer persuaded the authorities to allow tracks to cross Kent Avenue at North Fifth Street to a newly built brick depot three stories high, running to Wythe Avenue. This was later enlarged to the next block to accommodate the New York Central and the Hudson & West Shore railroads—all on Havemeyers & Elder-owned property. The single exception was the waterfront block between

North Fourth and North Fifth streets owned by the Pennsylvania Railroad. The railroad could not cross Kent Avenue, however, as Havemeyers & Elder owned the next inland parcel. In 1883, the *Brooklyn Daily Eagle* wrote:

> On the north side of North Fifth Street is Mr. Havemeyer's freight depot, which he placed at the exclusive use of the Erie Railroad. The other refiners in that section and businessmen generally ship and receive freight at this very important station of the Erie. It is said it ranks fourth among the freight depots of that road. The depot has become such an important one that it is now altogether too small, but no doubt Mr. Havemeyer will extend it a block further east.

He did.

Palmer also developed the Palmer Cooperage Company to service all the refineries. This he sold to Havemeyers & Elder in 1873. It was located in the block between North Fourth and North Fifth streets, Wythe and Kent avenues next to the rail depot. The *Brooklyn Daily Eagle*, describing it, wrote:

> Beside the great refining and storage establishments, Mr. Havemeyer controls the vast cooperage interests ... which is familiarly known as Palmer's Cooper Shop.

Palmer was not alone in the cooperage field. A German friend of William Dick named Paul Weidmann was also active in this business.* He had located between North Sixth and North Sev-

---

* Weidmann, born in Bavaria, Germany, in 1830, came to America in 1852. After a short apprenticeship in New York, he established a cooperage business in Williamsburgh in 1859. In addition to cooperage, he later established a brewery at North First Street and Berry Avenue that was operated by one of his sons. He was a director of the Germania Savings Bank, a member of the Merchant's Club, and a Freemason of Brooklyn. He died in 1896 at his home at 73 South Ninth Street, a block from his neighbor, Dick.

enth streets west of Kent Avenue and near the Dick refinery on North Seventh Street. After the Dick refinery had burned, the Sugar Trust bought the Weidmann Cooperage plant. Weidmann moved to North Eleventh Street and Wythe Avenue to reestablish his business. He was a major factor in cooperage. There was no monopoly in the 1870s. Stiles lists forty-two separate cooperage establishments in Brooklyn in that era. Among the largest were Havemeyers & Elder (later called the Brooklyn Cooperage Company), DeCastro & Donner, the Brooklyn Sugar Refining Company interests, and Paul Weidmann.

In 1874, it must have appeared to Havemeyers & Elder that both transportation and cooperage were getting out of hand. In that year they formed both the Brooklyn Eastern District Terminal and the Brooklyn Cooperage Company and made Lowell M. Palmer the general manager of these wholly-owned subsidiaries. The Brooklyn Eastern District Terminal was organized for the purpose of providing to shippers and receivers a single railroad company through which to do business from the Eastern District section of Brooklyn. It transported the goods to and from the main line railroad terminals on the Jersey shore and received a percentage of the total freight rate charged the shipper or receiver. During the years after 1874, Palmer negotiated an agreement with the seven trunk-line railroads that only the Brooklyn Eastern District Terminal would service customers from Newtown Creek south, including the Brooklyn Navy Yard in Wallabout Bay. The ace card was, of course, the fact that Havemeyers & Elder owned all the available land. The great Erie depot mentioned above also became part of the Brooklyn Eastern District Terminal depots. By 1887 the Brooklyn Eastern District Terminal achieved a monopoly of railroad service to the entire area. In 1890 Palmer was made its president, recognizing the fact that he had acted as such all along.

The Brooklyn Cooperage Company, also formed by Havemeyers & Elder, was organized to combine several different cooperage businesses both in Brooklyn and in New Jersey. In addition to

Above, view of North 3rd Street and *below*, North 2nd Street property, formerly part of the DeCastro and Donner refinery, c. 1911.

"Palmer's" cooperage and Weidmann's cooperage, a similar business in Greenpoint next to the Havemeyer Sugar Refining Company was acquired. Although not a complete monopoly, Brooklyn Cooperage became so dominant in the field that others gradually dropped out or joined it. After 1887 the company acquired large tracts of timberland in Arkansas and Missouri and operated stave plants in several locations. By 1910 it controlled the barrel business as completely as the Sugar Trust controlled the sugar business, with plants in all refining ports on the east and gulf coasts. Lowell M. Palmer had been extremely successful and was president of this company as well.

In 1887 when the Sugar Trust was organized, the partners of Havemeyers & Elder contributed to it their refinery in Brooklyn. They also contributed their subsidiary company, the Brooklyn Cooperage Company. They retained in their partnership, however, all the real estate they owned north of North Third Street and the Brooklyn Eastern District Terminal, which operated on much of this property. In fact, after the Dick & Meyer refinery burned and was demolished, Palmer acquired that site as well for Havemeyers & Elder, so by 1890 it owned an unbroken line of waterfront (except for the Pennsylvania Railroad block) from North Third to North Tenth streets. It is not possible to know for certain why the two senior partners, Theodore A. and Henry O. Havemeyer, chose to retain this real estate asset for themselves and their heirs. That it was extremely profitable was certain, and it is likely that their fascination with real estate (they both were to invest in Manhattan real estate in a major way later on) led them to believe that real estate, rather than sugar, was the priceless gem to be retained in the family.

A third subsidiary company, also run by Palmer, was the Brooklyn Transportation Company. This concern delivered sugar locally. It operated stables in Brooklyn and maintained a fleet of wagons. The stables accommodated three hundred horses and contained a sick ward under the supervision of a veterinary, as well as blacksmith and harness shops.

Lowell M. Palmer, the principal figure in charge of all the cooperage and transportation for the Sugar Trust, was made a director of the American Sugar Refining Company in 1899, one of only seven. He had secured very favorable freight rates for the Brooklyn Eastern District Terminal and very favorable advantages for the Brooklyn Cooperage Company. He had "earned his wings" and the confidence of Henry O. Havemeyer. In fact, in 1900, when the National Sugar Refining Company was organized (see Chapter 5), H.O. Havemeyer placed his common shares in a voting trust for five years and named Palmer to be the only other trustee with him, certainly a sign of great trust. This relationship lasted only until 1902, however, when a complete breach occurred. At that time Havemeyer considered selling his National Sugar shares to the American Sugar Refining Company. At a special meeting of the American Sugar Refining Company board held on March 4 that year, a committee consisting of directors Senff, Thomas, and Palmer was authorized to investigate the desirability of purchasing these shares for the company. (The meeting was held at One East 66th Street, Havemeyer's home.) Two weeks later the committee, including Palmer, approved the purchase and authorized the treasurer to consult counsel as to the best means of so doing. Palmer admitted later (1911) that he had been in favor of the purchase provided it was put before the shareholders for approval. He said that Mr. Havemeyer did not agree to this, and therefore he, Palmer, declined to vote for the purchase unless the company counsel, John G. Johnson,* would advise in favor of it on the basis of appropriateness and legality. Palmer agreed to follow Johnson's advice, but the latter recommended against it. In May 1902 the treasurer reported that Mr. Havemeyer did not care to pursue the matter. He had decided to retain the shares for himself and his family.

Palmer believed that this incident had earned him the lasting

---

* Johnson, known as "king of the American bar," had previously defended the company from attack by both federal and state governments and pleaded its case before the Supreme Court in the E. C. Knight case (see Chapter 5).

Logging, *above*, and the stave mills, *below*, in Poplar Bluff, Missouri, c. 1911, owned and operated by Brooklyn Cooperage Company to produce barrels for shipping sugar.

enmity of H. O. Havemeyer. He claimed that he stayed on as president of the three subsidiaries only because he had a contract to do so. However, at that same time (March 1902), Havemeyer discovered and reported to his board that Palmer secretly owned timberlands from which lumber was sold to the Brooklyn Cooperage Company. To remove this conflict of interest he required Palmer to sell these lands (93,000 acres) to Brooklyn Cooperage at low prices. Then later in 1905 he suspected Palmer of forming a competing lumber company at Poplar Bluff, Missouri, where Brooklyn Cooperage had some of its timberlands. Palmer resigned from the American Sugar Refining Company board in January 1905 and in July 1906 as president of the Brooklyn Cooperage Company, the Brooklyn Eastern District Terminal, and the Brooklyn Transportation Company.

After leaving the Sugar Trust, Palmer, aged sixty-one, started a new career as a founder and first president of E. R. Squibb & Sons, the pharmaceutical house. He remained in that position until his death in 1915. He also retained a substantial interest in waterfront property in Brooklyn through the Palmer Waterfront Land and Improvement Company. A longtime resident of the borough, he had a summer house as well in Stamford, Connecticut, near the home of his former colleague, H. O. Havemeyer.

After Palmer's departure in 1906, Henry O. Havemeyer asked his deceased brother's son, also called Henry O. Havemeyer, to become president of the Brooklyn Eastern District Terminal. Henry had been trained in the family fashion in the Havemeyers & Elder refinery and in the office of the American Sugar Refining Company. He remained the Brooklyn Eastern District Terminal president until 1957—fifty-one years. The family firm of Havemeyers & Elder, owning that "priceless" real estate in the Eastern District, was also controlled by H. O. Havemeyer's son Horace, after the senior's death in 1907. Those two cousins guided its fortunes for the next half century.

William Dick's interests in real estate in the Eastern District were of a very different nature from those of the Havemeyers. As previously mentioned, when the Dick & Meyer sugar refinery went into the Sugar Trust in 1887, the partners received a large amount of stock, which became American Sugar Refining Company stock. When Dick died twenty-five years later, he owned only a very few shares of this stock. In this he was very much like his friend Henry O. Havemeyer. Dick's estate of approximately $4 million was diversified among mortgages, bonds, stocks, and real estate. Only $250,000 was in American Sugar Refining preferred and common stock. It is interesting to note that two of the mortgages owned by the estate represented loans to the German Evangelical Lutheran Trinity Church of Long Island City and to the Evangelical Lutheran Church on Degraw Street in downtown Brooklyn (see Chapter 8).

Although diversified, Dick's estate had a definite character reflecting his activity in business over his final twenty-five years. Many of the mortgages were to individuals located in Williamsburgh—in most cases, mortgages on their homes. Many of the bonds and stocks represented investments in local public enterprises, such as Citizens Water Supply Company (this was to become Citizens Development Company, held in the family today). Other investments were in several Brooklyn transit companies and a utility company. An investment in the Cord Meyer Development Company, the family interest of his former sugar partner, Cord Meyer, represented real estate development in Brooklyn and then Queens. There were several sugar company stocks and bonds, most likely investments made at Havemeyer's suggestion. There was the stock of his bank, then called the Manufacturer's-Citizens Trust Company. Finally, there were investments in some thirty parcels of real estate, all but one or two in the Williamsburgh section, concentrated along Broadway and along Bedford Avenue—the city center in 1912. He also owned most of the houses on South Ninth Street (148-165 South Ninth Street), the block where he lived.

From this it is possible to conclude that Dick's business was essentially local, involving real estate, backing small public enterprises or people in the manner a local savings bank would do today. Entrepreneurial in nature, this business would have demanded active daily management, which it received from Dick until his retirement at the age of eighty-four in 1907.

The Lutheran Church of the Redeemer, the church John Henry Dick and his family attended from 1897 to 1906. The building minus the spire and the cross stands today.

8

The Lutheran Church and Other Philanthropic Endeavors (1853-1912)

William Dick, John Mollenhauer, and their wives were all of German Lutheran heritage and played an active role in the development of that church in the Eastern District. We should first look briefly at the history of the Lutherans in America prior to the mid-nineteenth century.

A Lutheran church did exist in Manhattan in Dutch times, but it was tiny and remained so until after the Revolutionary War. In fact the only pastor was a royalist who had to flee to Nova Scotia when the English evacuated New York in 1783. Subsequently a new pastor was found and the church grew slowly until around 1815, when a conflict developed that was to plague the church for years to come—whether services should be in German or in the new tongue, English. As most Lutherans were first-generation immigrants who spoke only German, the German-language Evangelical Lutherans became dominant and remained so throughout the entire nineteenth century.

Because the only Lutheran church in Manhattan in 1815 had German services, a new "large and spacious" church was erected in 1821 at 79 Walker Street near Broadway. It was called Saint Matthew's. English services were held there at first, but soon public pressure forced a change to German, and from 1840 on only German was spoken at Saint Matthew's. Pastor C. F. E. Stohlmann led the congregation at that time, and it was he who conducted the weddings of both the Dicks and the Mollenhauers at Saint Matthew's.

In Brooklyn during the 1840s there was no Lutheran church at all, so worshipers had to go to Saint Matthew's in Manhattan. As increasing numbers of Germans began to settle in Dutchtown in Williamsburgh, congregations, with the active encouragement of Pastor Stohlmann, gathered for worship in local residences and pastors came from Manhattan to preach. In 1847 the German Evangelical Congregation was formed and worshiped in a public school. In 1849 a lot was purchased at the corner of Graham Avenue and Ten Eyck Street, where a church building was built and dedicated. In December 1853 its name became the German Evangelical Lutheran St. John's Congregation. Among the first members of its council was William Dick, who had moved to Williamsburgh that year. Thirty years later in 1883, a block or so away on Maujer Street near Humboldt Street, the cornerstone was laid for a new brick church building in pure Gothic style with a belfry and a 165-foot spire. The old building became a parochial school. Dick served on the church council for fifty-three years and was a major benefactor of the new building, as he was of many other Lutheran institutions. St. John's remained a German-speaking congregation throughout Dick's lifetime, and at his funeral, which was held in his home (that being the custom then), the service was conducted in German by the St. John's pastor, the Reverend Beyer, while the eulogy was given in English by the Reverend Koepschen of the Lutheran Church on 42nd Street in Manhattan.

The large immigration of German Lutherans after 1848, many of whom settled in Williamsburgh, brought about the need for more churches there. Several were organized in the early 1850s. In addition to St. John's, St. Paul's Evangelical Lutheran Church was founded in 1853. The first meeting of that church board was held at the Grand Street residence of Mr. John W. Dick (William Dick's older brother) on May 5, 1853. St. Paul's was first located on Rodney Street and South First Street. Among the original trustees were John W. Dick and Lur Wintjen, the first treasurer. William Dick was listed as treasurer in 1860. In 1884, St. Paul's moved to Rodney Street and South Fifth Street. The committee for the new building consisted of Jost Moller, Lur Wintjen, and the two Claus Doschers, father and son. The sugar industry was well represented. Finally, in 1903, when the church celebrated its fiftieth anniversary, heading the list of the Honorary Jubilee Committee was Mr. Lur Wintjen, by then ninety years old, the only surviving member of the first church council.

As the population expanded, several other churches were formed in all parts of the Eastern District. In the fall of 1867 the Reverend Augustus Schubert gathered together several German families who had been attending services at a nearby hall and organized a congregation to be called the First German Evangelical Lutheran St. Peter's Church of Brooklyn, New York. The church was first located on DeKalb Avenue and later moved to Bedford Avenue near DeKalb, where a new church building was erected in 1887. John Mollenhauer, whose first home in Brooklyn was on nearby Marcy Avenue near Hart Street, was elected a trustee in 1868. He remained a trustee throughout his life, despite the fact that when he moved his residence to Ross Street, the trip to church became a much longer one, over a mile. St. Peter's was notable for breaking a firm tradition. Under the long-term pastorate of Dr. John J. Heischmann (1879-1928) there was introduced, against some opposition, an English-language service on Sunday evenings. This was the first English service in a German Lutheran church in Brooklyn. Mollenhauer was a major benefactor of St. Peter's and substantially helped the church rebuild in 1887.

> On Sunday May 22, 1898, the mortgage for $30,000 was burned at the altar at the morning service by Mr. John Mollenhauer, whose great liberality together with the energetic work of the Ladies Aid Society was a salient factor in clearing the debt. (*History of St. Peter's Church*, 1913)

After his death, Mollenhauer's funeral was conducted in his home by his longtime friend and pastor Dr. Heischmann, on the evening of January 3, 1905. Several years later in the St. Peter's annual report the following note appeared:

> The year 1910 is noteworthy by the exquisite gift presented to the Church by one of its members. In loving memory of her departed husband, the late John Mollenhauer, Mrs. Doris Mollenhauer presented the church with a set of eleven bells which on April 10 of that year were consecrated by our pastor.

The language question was becoming an increasing problem for the Lutheran Church in America, as the century drew to a close. Most German Lutheran congregations were insisting that the mother tongue be retained and that the surrender of the language was a surrender of their heritage of which they were intensely proud. Increasingly the second- and third-generation German Americans spoke English as their primary language. They wanted to worship with the English service and still remain part of the Lutheran church. The result was tension. Some congregations adopted the practice of having some English services, as St. Peter's did, but often the pastor, educated in Germany and knowing only German, could not preach in English. As a result of this tension, English-language Lutheran churches began to form even in the mostly Germanic communities such as Williamsburgh.* In 1894 a small group of the St. Paul's congregation on Rodney Street met to form a new congregation, worshiping in the English language only. Thirty-six teachers resigned to become members of this new congregation and to start its Sunday school. The church was called the Evangelical Lutheran Church of the Redeemer, and a new church building was completed at the end of 1896 on the corner of Bedford Avenue and Hewes Street. The congregation soon numbered five hundred, with five hundred children in its Sunday school. Among the children were John Henry and Julia Dick's two

---

* By the 1870s this tension was also occurring in Manhattan.

sons and two daughters. They attended classes there about a half mile from their home on South Ninth Street. Daughters Doris and Julia were confirmed there on Sunday, April 8, 1906, even though the family had moved to Manhattan two years earlier. A stained-glass window was given to the church by their parents to commemorate the occasion.

The Dicks remained Lutherans through the third generation, being associated in Manhattan with Trinity Lutheran Church on 65th Street and Central Park West, the pastorate of the Reverend Paul Scherer.

Other Philanthropic Endeavors

William Dick took a particularly active interest in hospitals. Brooklyn historian Dr. Brockett said, "He is connected as trustee with the Charitable Hospital, the Third Street Dispensary and as treasurer with the German Lutheran Hospital of East New York" (1884).

The Third Street Dispensary dates back to 1851, although it changed its name to the Eastern District Dispensary at the time of the district's consolidation. In 1880 a new building was erected for its use on South Third Street between Berry and Bedford. Somewhat later the dispensary became known as the Williamsburgh Hospital and was expanded by the addition of a wing in 1892. An involvement with three hospitals would not have been unusual for the successful immigrant merchant of that time, particularly with so many German and Lutheran institutions coming into being. There could not have been many men available who had the interest and qualifications to serve these institutions.

Dick and Mollenhauer were members of three clubs—the Hanover Club, the Merchant's Club, and the Eastern District Club. The Hanover Club, a "gentlemen's club," was organized in 1890. The original directors, who included John Henry Dick and J. Adolph Mollenhauer, purchased the Hawley mansion at the

Left, John Henry Dick (1851-1925), the only son of William Dick. He was an original director of the Hanover Club, *below*, at the corner of Bedford Avenue and Rodney Street, c. 1911.

corner of Bedford Avenue and Rodney Street just a block and a half from Mollenhauer's home on Ross Street. The mansion was remodeled and enlarged to provide the membership with facilities for bowling, rathskeller, billiards, and whist. Members were the socially prominent men of that time. The first president of the club was William Cullen Bryant (1849-1905), publisher of the *Brooklyn Times* and namesake of the poet.

The Merchant's Club was organized earlier, in the winter of 1880-81, by some forty people who had withdrawn from the Union Club. It was located at 95 South Tenth Street and was said to be "tinged with the spirit of conservatism" (*Brooklyn Daily Eagle*). It never became as large as the Hanover Club. Perhaps it was even more exclusive. That both Dick and Mollenhauer and their sons were members in good standing of both these clubs confirms that they had achieved social respectability as leading citizens of Brooklyn.

The Eastern District Club was a political club. It is doubtful that Dick and Mollenhauer were much involved in the political life of their city, although both they and their sons were listed in 1890 as club members. Although they never held elective offices, Mollenhauer was one of the first of the Brooklyn Bridge commissioners and served on both the executive and finance committees of this board. Mollenhauer was also a Freemason* of Brooklyn and served for five years as treasurer of the Euclid Lodge on Bedford Avenue. William Dick was a life member of the Brooklyn Institute of Arts and Sciences.

Williamsburgh—or the Eastern District, as it was called by then—was changing rapidly as the century drew to a close. Two events marked the change. In 1898 the City of Brooklyn, entirely independent until then, was merged into the City of New York. Perhaps more symbolic than practical, the move meant that Brooklyn was losing an identity, at least to those who did not live

---

* Free and Accepted Mason is the full title of the order.

there. Second, and more critical to the Eastern District, the Williamsburgh Bridge, having been started in 1896, was opened in December 1903.* This new connection to Manhattan caused the old center city of Williamsburgh to move eastward again along Broadway to the newly created bridge plaza, bounded by Driggs Avenue on the west and Havemeyer Street on the east. It also speeded the migration to Manhattan of some of the older Williamsburgh residents who feared the loss of the village aspects or who wanted to be located near their successful peers in Manhattan.

John Henry and Julia Dick were among those who migrated to Manhattan. In the spring of 1904 they purchased a newly built townhouse at 20 East 53rd Street between Madison and Fifth avenues in Manhattan. Alterations were made over the summer, and by fall the house was ready for the family to move in, just in time for daughters Doris and Julia to attend the Spence School. The *Brooklyn Daily Eagle* described the house:

> It is built of yellow brick and white stone of the American basement type, a French exterior in its architecture, modified to be in harmony with Manhattan conditions. Four stories high, it has ample room space for entertaining, and by a clever arrangement of the floors, space for a large corps of servants to move from floor to floor and get speedily in attendance without passing through the hallways and up the main flight of stairs. The typical house of Society is such a one as Mr. Dick has purchased, and he has secured an exceptionally spacious and fine representative.**

---

* The Brooklyn Bridge was the first large suspension bridge built anywhere. It paved the way for the Williamsburgh Bridge.

** Three floors of the original facade remain. The old building, now used for offices, has been extended upward by three stories to provide additional space.

Although the transition from Brooklyn to Manhattan was almost complete, the family traveled on most Sundays to visit grandfather Dick and grandmother Mollenhauer in Brooklyn and continued attending church there.

While the John Henry Dicks moved across the river, none of the Mollenhauer sons of the second generation ever did.* They remained in Brooklyn, although they all eventually moved out of the old Williamsburgh area to more suitable parts of the borough.

---

*   Frederick D. Mollenhauer's residence, a handsome neo-renaissance limestone mansion, was built in 1896 at 505 Bedford Avenue at the corner of Taylor Street, two blocks from his father's home on Ross Street. It still stands today and is used as a Hasidic Yeshiva.

Above, two views of the Williamsburgh Bridge. *Bottom*, looking north up the East River. The Havemeyers & Elder refinery complex is just beyond the bridge on the right, c. 1905.

9

The Eastern District
of Brooklyn in 1907

John Mollenhauer, born in Ebersdorf, Germany, seventy-seven years before, died on December 31, 1904, at his long-time residence, 156 Ross Street in Williamsburgh. He had been active until the end. The *New York Times* described his death as "sudden." It went on to say:

> He bought tickets yesterday for Summerville, South Carolina, where he had an estate, meaning to leave New York on January 10th and spending the rest of the winter there with his family. He went driving with Mrs. Mollenhauer in Prospect Park in the afternoon and upon his return went to the Merchant's Club of which he was a member. While there he complained of feeling ill. He went home and Dr. Essig of 488 Bedford Avenue, the family physician, was called. He died of apoplexy [most likely cerebral hemorrhage] soon after that.

He was survived by his wife of fifty-one years, Doris (who died in 1915, aged eighty-five), by a daughter, Julia T. Dick, and four sons, J. William, J. Adolph, Frederick D., and Henry F. Mollenhauer.

He was described in this obituary as the sugar refiner who fought the Sugar Trust consistently until 1900 when his business was combined into the National Sugar Refining Company (see Chapter 5). This very brief description does not really do justice to the life of a man who came from a foreign country, penniless, speaking no English, yet became a successful merchant and a leading citizen in his community. Perhaps that is fitting after all, because he never sought the limelight. As has been seen, he chose to co-exist with but not to fight the Sugar Trust, undoubtedly an act of wisdom in those days. Although he was a leading merchant and banker in Williamsburgh, there is no evidence he was involved in political life, probably because those of Germanic background and language were not looked to for leadership until much later. A Williamsburgh German-language newspaper concluded an article about him at the time of his death:

> Mr. Mollenhauer's goals were not only directed toward financial success. On the contrary, always concerned for the community, he possessed those rare qualities of an outstanding citizen which made our Republic what it is today.

Mollenhauer's death was the first among his generation of sugar merchants in the Eastern District of Brooklyn.

On December 4, 1907, at his farm in Commack, Long Island, where he had gone for Thanksgiving to hunt pheasants, Henry O. Havemeyer, at age sixty, died suddenly of acute nephritis. He was survived by his wife of twenty-four years, Louisine Waldron, by a son, Horace, and two daughters, Adaline and Electra. He was the youngest son in a large family whose head, Frederick C. Havemeyer Jr. had become the preeminent sugar refiner in America by the mid-nineteenth century. From a background of privilege, Henry O., through study and application and using a genius for financial organization and commercial merchandising, became the central figure in the sugar industry. He dominated that industry throughout the country from 1890 until his death, in the way that John D. Rockefeller dominated the oil industry before him. The Sugar Trust, as his creation was known, covered most of America, but its heart and soul remained in Williamsburgh at the huge Havemeyers & Elder refinery on Kent Avenue. Although the Havemeyers never lived in Brooklyn, their commercial interests in Williamsburgh were the largest in the area, providing livelihood for hundreds of Williamsburgh residents.

John Mollenhauer (1827-1904), senior citizen of Williamsburgh.

It is possible to claim that an era ended in 1907 with H. O Havemeyer's death, for William Dick retired from active business that year as well. His wife of fifty years, Anna, had died in 1898, aged seventy-eight. His daughter and son-in-law who lived nearby must have looked in on him often at his home at 156 South Ninth Street. His son and daughter-in-law had moved to Manhattan but visited Williamsburgh regularly every Sunday with their four children. One of them, Doris Anna Dick, remembered kissing him with his full beard. He had written his last will in 1906, providing that his affairs be looked after by both his son, J. Henry Dick, and his son-in-law, J. Adolph Mollenhauer. His grandson William K. Dick was also involved with his affairs by then. On April 5, 1912, William Dick died at the extraordinary age of eighty-nine. The *New York Times* said he "had been failing rapidly for several months." He was described as a "sugar refinery pioneer," born in Hannover, Germany, who became "one of the largest stockholders of the American Sugar Refinery Company and a director thereof." Unlike many in the nineteenth century who became rich after a penniless immigrant start, Dick remained in the place he knew best, Williamsburgh. He had devoted his life to the development of that area. Dr. Brockett said:

> Retired and domestic in his tastes and habits, he shrinks from rather than seeks publicity. With his disposition he is content to discharge the citizen's duty at the ballot box, without seeking political preferment; though his modesty cannot conceal the fact that he is one of the leading influential men of the Eastern District and so recognized everywhere. He is respected for his intrinsic worth as a man, and beloved by those who have received his benefactions. He enjoys the comforts of an elegant house with the wife of his youth. They do their part in society, and their house is frequently opened to their large circle of friends. Mr. Dick has already attained to a great degree of usefulness; but with every year his business relations,

Henry O. Havemeyer, c. 1898.

> his charities and his influence expand, so that the
> future alone can reveal to what he may yet come.

Written in 1884 almost thirty years before his death, this article could well have served as his obituary.

What did Williamsburgh look like at the end of this era, in 1907? The waterfront was not too different from its appearance in earlier times. Still dominating the skyline was the Havemeyers & Elder sugar refinery, now owned by the American Sugar Refining Company. Alongside it loomed the newly completed Williamsburgh Bridge. To the south were several ferry docks still active in spite of the bridge, the Brooklyn Distilling Company, and the closed Mollenhauer refinery of the National Sugar Refining Company. The view ended with Wallabout Bay and the Brooklyn Navy Yard, which was rapidly expanding to become one of the largest on the east coast. Well beyond to the south the Arbuckle plant continued to refine sugar as it had for the past nine years.

To the north of the Havemeyers & Elder refinery was property owned by the American Sugar Refining Company on which the DeCastro & Donner plant still stood (it was now used as a warehouse for sugar) and a factory of the Brooklyn Cooperage Company. The adjacent block of North Fourth to North Fifth Street, owned by the Pennsylvania Railroad, was followed by five blocks of Havemeyers & Elder property on which the Brooklyn Eastern District Terminal operated. Also on this property was another factory of Brooklyn Cooperage, as well as Palmer's Hay Sheds and Palmer's Coal Pocket. At North Twelfth Street and Bushwick Creek was the Pratt Oil Works,* established in 1867, the first oil refinery located in New York.

---

* The founder, Charles Pratt (1830-1891), came to New York from Massachusetts to build what was considered at the time the model refinery in the oil industry. This was because it produced a high grade of kerosene for lamps that was less apt to explode than most competing fuels. In 1874, Pratt sold out to the Standard Oil Company of John D. Rockefeller and became a major partner and the wealthiest man in Brooklyn. He founded the Pratt Institute for the training of skilled artisans, designers, and draftsmen. In spite of his great wealth he continued to live modestly on Clinton Avenue in Brooklyn.

Finally, along Newtown Creek at the north of the Greenpoint section, the old Havemeyer sugar refinery had just been dismantled, but the American Sugar Refining Company still owned the site. Across the creek the Long Island City refinery of the National, under the management of J. Henry Lienau, was operating in good order.

To the east and moving inland, the Manufacturers National Bank with Dick's office was still at the corner of Broadway and Berry Street. A block away, the Dime Savings Bank of Williamsburgh, Mollenhauer's bank, was still on the corner of Broadway and Wythe Avenue, although it was about to move to Havemeyer Street in the next year. On South Ninth Street stood the Dick residences, across from the Lutheran Emmanuel Church. On Ross Street was John Mollenhauer's brownstone home a block from the Hanover Club.

After 1907, a new century had begun and a new generation of leaders had taken over in the sugar, transportation, and banking businesses in the Eastern District of Brooklyn. Among them were sons and later grandsons of H.O. Havemeyer and Theodore A. Havemeyer, William Dick and John Mollenhauer. H.O.'s son, Horace; his grandsons Horace Jr. and Harry Waldron; Theodore's son, Henry O.; William Dick's grandson, William K. Dick; and John Mollenhauer's sons, J. Adolph, Frederick D., and Henry F., would become active in these businesses.

During the latter half of the nineteenth century, the lives of three families had interconnected in the course of pursuing the business of refining sugar in the part of Brooklyn first known as Williamsburgh and later as the Eastern District. These families had a major impact on the area at that time. They should be remembered among the builders of a new city in a new nation.

Above, the Havemeyers & Elder refinery complex in 1905, prior to the death of H. O. Havemeyer. It was then the "jewel in the crown" of the Sugar Trust. *Below* the Havemeyers & Elder refinery in 1988, called the Amstar Corporation, maker of Domino brand sugar. The raw sugar unloading dock is on the left and the refined sugar warehouse is on the right. The brick building with the smokestack in between them is all that remains from the old refinery. The rest of the refinery is modern. The Williamsburgh Bridge is on the far right.

The Eastern District
of Brooklyn in 1987

If one was to travel through Williamsburgh today looking for signs of that past time of industrial expansion, one would be hard pressed to find many. Indeed, signs of decay are everywhere, from the waterfront to the old center city of the 1880s. Driving up Kent Avenue, one finds the Brooklyn Navy Yard closed and a new industrial complex struggling to get started in Wallabout Bay. The F. & M. Schaefer brewery on the Mollenhauer refinery site is also closed. The lots where the ferry docks were located are empty. Only after passing under the Williamsburgh Bridge is one's quest rewarded. The old Havemeyers & Elder refinery, entirely modernized inside, still remains and produces Domino sugar for Amstar Corporation, its present owner and successor to the American Sugar Refining Company. Northward beyond the giant oil tanks of the New England Petroleum Company, the Austin Nichols building, built by Havemeyers & Elder in 1914 as a warehouse, appears in use. The Pennsylvania Railroad block is a scrap metal yard filled with crushed cars and other junk. Finally, the Havemeyers & Elder Brooklyn Eastern District Terminal property north of North Fifth Street is completely silent. Its few warehouses and office building are abandoned, broken, and burned-out hulks. As a result of railroad bankruptcy, nothing of value is left at all. That waterfront land, the "priceless gem" of past times, is now owned by the City of New York, which took it over in lieu of unpaid taxes. It is available to any interested buyer. The Pratt Oil Works have long disappeared as well, and there are no sugar refineries to the north anymore, the Long Island City plant of National Sugar Refining Company having been closed in 1964. In fact the Havemeyers &

Elder refinery is one of only two refineries operating in all of New York harbor.*

Driving inland along Broadway, one finds a few of the century-old buildings remaining, as if to proclaim a grandeur that has gone. There is the bank building at the corner of Berry Street, five stories high with distinguished columns alongside the corner entrance door, but without its original dome. One can easily picture William Dick walking in to work in his office there in the morning. Its ground floor is now a branch of the Manufacturers Hanover Bank. In the next block at the Bedford Avenue corner is the five-story white sandstone building of the old Nassau Trust Company on the south side and the three-story Kings County Savings Bank building on the north, both now used for other purposes. At Driggs Avenue the Williamsburgh Savings Bank (built in 1875) with its distinctive domed roof is still the dominant feature in the skyline of the Williamsburgh Plaza. Finally, at Havemeyer Street the Dime Savings Bank remains open for the thrifty where it moved in 1908 after Mollenhauer's death. Broadway is a wide street in these blocks, merging into the Plaza and the elevated subway coming from the bridge. There are no modern buildings at all, a testament to decline.

South of Broadway to South Ninth Street and Driggs Avenue the scene becomes even more depressing. The Dick houses on that block have long been torn down.** The apartment building that re-

---

*   The second is in Yonkers on the Hudson River. It is owned by the British refiner Tate & Lyle PLC.

**   In 1925 the *Brooklyn Daily Eagle* said:
The Dick mansion and two adjoining buildings at South Ninth Street and Driggs Avenue, landmarks of the Eastern District and scene of many social events a generation ago, will be demolished to make way for an apartment building .... The builders expect to raze the old structure in the fall. Some time ago the mansion and the two adjoining buildings were secured by the Board of Directors of the old Williamsburgh Hospital as a site for a new hospital and a movement was started to raise funds for the purpose. The plan was eventually abandoned. Later on the mansion was used as a home by the nurses of the Williamsburgh Hospital and finally the building was closed because of much-needed repairs.

placed them, called the Mayflower, is occupied, but much in need of repair after a fire in one part of the structure. With many shell buildings nearby, the area is reminiscent of the worst of the South Bronx today.

Further south still to Ross Street, one enters the principal Hasidic neighborhood of New York City. Here, surprisingly, still stands the Mollenhauers' handsome four-story brownstone house with attractive stonework along its cornice. How many times John and Doris Mollenhauer must have walked up and down those steps! Around the corner in the next block the mansion that was the Hanover Club, with its rounded corner turret, upstairs porch, and carved stone decoration, is used by the Hasidim. Also remaining is the Frederick D. Mollenhauer mansion on Bedford Avenue and Taylor Street, a charming Victorian-style house with two chimneys, a copper cornice, and a handsome entrance porch with Corinthian columns. It is today a Yeshiva (Yeshiva Yesoda Hatora of Khaladas Veriam). On Saturday one sees the faithful going to temple—men in knickers, long coats, and fur caps all in black; women, all with hats on, pushing baby carriages; and children trailing after, the boys like the men with the single long curl hanging down in front of each ear. There are also some new apartment buildings along Bedford Avenue to house this thriving community.

St. Peter's German Lutheran Church with its Mollenhauer bells is gone from Bedford and DeKalb avenues. The Church of the Redeemer on Bedford and Hewes, where the Dick children went to Sunday school, its spire and its crosses removed, is now used as an Hasidic school for girls (Beth-Chana School for Girls). St. Paul's German Lutheran Church on South Fifth and Rodney streets, now connected with the Lutheran Church of America, has services for the mainly Hispanic people of that area. Finally St. John's German Lutheran, William Dick's church on Maujer Street, still stands. The date 1883 and its name in German are inscribed on the brick beneath the belfry tower and the 165-foot spire, which were reconstructed following a fire ten years ago. It is now called

St. John the Evangelist and is associated with the Missouri Synod of the Lutherans. Until the early 1970s German-language services were held at St. John's. Today the service on Sunday in English is held in the neighboring center in the winter for lack of heat in the church itself. There has been no organ since the fire. Clearly St. John's on Maujer Street is near the end of its life. The St. John's school next door holds classes for a few neighborhood children, some forty or fifty.

Much of the Eastern District might be called an area in transition. It is today at the nadir of a curve. There are large amounts of land to develop both on the waterfront and inland. When will the next entrepreneurs come along? The space and the labor are as available today as they were in 1850. Will the cycle repeat itself? Only time will tell.

Green-Wood Cemetery, opened in 1840, is a vast necropolis in a park-like setting on the Gowanus Heights of Brooklyn overlooking the Upper Bay of New York harbor. The Statue of Liberty is clearly seen in the distance. It is entered through a majestic Gothic Revival gateway designed by Richard Upjohn, the notable church architect,* and built of brownstone. The structure is set back several hundred feet from the street, increasing its prominence as one approaches. A writer of the 1890s observed of Green-Wood:

> All that wealth can command, everything that
> taste can suggest, all that local pride can bestow
> has been lavished in the efforts to beautify this
> silent city.

It is set on historic ground as well. Within is Battle Hill, the site of the Battle of Long Island, the first military engagement of the United States after July 4, 1776. To mark this spot, the Altar to Liberty, a statue of the goddess Athena, was erected. She stands with her arm uplifted in perpetual salute to the Statue of Liberty across the Bay.

---

*   The architect of present-day Trinity Church on Wall Street.

Above, the Mollenhauers' mausoleum and, *below*, the Havemeyers' Orchard Hill vault, both at Green-Wood Cemetery.

Frederick C. Havemeyer, his wife, Catherine Billiger, their son Frederick C. Havemeyer Jr. and grandson Henry O. Havemeyer were all buried together with many of their offspring in Green-Wood Cemetery, although none had ever lived in Brooklyn. In a high section of the cemetery a large grassy knoll was purchased by Catherine Billiger Havemeyer in 1854, and she had her husband's and her father's remains moved there. It is called Orchard Hill and overlooks the Upper Bay of New York harbor—a beautiful site. Their graves are all in an underground mausoleum marked simply at the entrance with the name HAVEMEYER.

John Mollenhauer, his wife, Doris, their four sons William, Adolph, Frederick, and Henry, and Adolph's wife, Anna M. Dick, were all buried in Green-Wood Cemetery as well. A classic Greek mausoleum with four Doric columns, modeled after the Athenian Treasury at Delphi, stands in a sylvan setting amidst tall trees along "Pilgrim Path." The name MOLLENHAUER is carved in the marble on the front. It, like the other, is an eminently peaceful resting place.

William Dick, his wife, Anna, their son John Henry and daughter-in-law Julia T. (Mollenhauer), their grandsons, William K. and Adolph M. Dick, were all buried in the old Lutheran cemetery on Metropolitan Avenue just across the Brooklyn line in Queens. At the time of John Henry Dick's death in 1925, a mausoleum was erected for him and his parents as well as for his wife who died in 1931. It was located on the side of the cemetery's Pleasant Hill. Due to disrepair, the mausoleum was torn down in 1953 prior to the burial of William K. Dick that year. All are buried today beneath the ground, their graves marked by simple stones engraved with names and dates of birth and death. Alongside the graves are two stones of remembrance designed in Victorian style with the names of the parents of Anna Vagts Dick: Claus Vagts, Geliebte Eltern von Anna M. Dick—Vater; and Christine Vagts Geliebte Cattin von William Dick—Mutter.

In the adjacent plot are the graves of William Dick's first business partner, Lur Wintjen, and his wife Margaretha Vagts Wintjen, Dick's sister-in-law. Slightly beyond are the graves of Dick's other German Lutheran friend, Paul Weidmann, the "cooper," and his family.

Above, the Domino plant in 2010, six years after it ceased operating. On the left is the refinery building and on the right the packaging plant with its iconic Domino Sugar sign. *Below*, the packaging plant, shortly before it was demolished, with sticky puddles on the floor and the smell of sugar permeating the air.

The Final Years
(1988-2004)

The final years of the sugar refinery on Kent Avenue in Williamsburgh, Brooklyn, that had been once called Havemeyers & Elder, then the American Sugar Refining Company and Amstar for short in 1988, underwent another change to Domino Sugar Corporation. The refinery had been purchased that year by the giant British sugar company Tate & Lyle Ltd. along with three other American refineries in Boston, Baltimore, and Chalmette, New Orleans. Tate & Lyle also had sugar interests in Canada. However, the sugar market was very tight in the decade of the 1990s and the refiners throughout the USA were in a bind. Owners were not making the profits that they counted on. There was more refining capacity in the US than was needed and the smaller refineries, such as the Boston one that Tate had just purchased, were closed down. In Philadelphia another Amstar refinery was closed as well. By 2001 officials at Tate & Lyle said, "they were selling their refineries because Domino is losing money on every pound of sugar it sells."

The headlines in the *St. Petersburg Times* on July 27, 2001, announced, "Florida Family to Acquire Domino Sugar Organization." The Florida family, the buyers, were the brothers Alfonso and Pepe Fanjul, sixty-four and fifty-seven years old, who had fled Cuba in 1959 when Castro came to power. They moved to Florida, investing in the sugar cane interests of U. S. Sugar Company around Lake Okeechobee in the southern part of the state. They had competed with Tate & Lyle in 1988 for refineries in the USA but lost out then. They also owned part of the refining business at Yonkers on the Hudson River in Westchester County, New York.

Although the Fanjuls were successful in 2001 in buying Tate & Lyle's three US refineries, the cost of operating the Brooklyn Domino plant was more that they could handle and the margin of profit was not there between raw and refined sugar. In 2004, after three years of suffering losses, the brothers announced the closing of the Brooklyn refinery in order to keep running the Baltimore one with a much newer plant. Thus for the first time since the refinery fire of 1882 the original Havemeyers & Elder plant was closed for good and dismantling was begun.

However, a new era would dawn for old refinery. In April 2017 the *Wall Street Journal* wrote an article titled "Domino Sugar Site Gets Makeover," describing a plan for the development of the property on Kent Avenue by Jed Walentas of Two Trees Management Inc. A sixteen-story residential building, the first building in the long-delayed $3 million project, opened in July 2017. A second residential building opened in 2019, with more planned to open in phases. A new waterfront park, called Domino Park, stretches along the East River. A playground imaginatively uses old equipment from the refinery. It is an attractive park for all to use. Today in 2022 only the main refinery building remains in place with new housing going up all around it. Landmarked in 2007, it will be converted to office space. Below the smokestack, on the west side of the building, is the old marking Havemeyers & Elder.

Children cool off in Domino Park's fountain in front of the old refinery building as it undergoes transformation to an office building during the summer of 2022.

Havemeyer Family Tree[*]

William Havemeyer
1770-1851
m. Susannah Clegg
1781-1838

William Frederick Havemeyer
1804-1874
m. Sarah Agnes Craig
1809-1896

Dietrick Wilhelm Hovemeyer
1725-1784

Frederick C. Havemeyer Jr.
1807-1891
m. Sarah Louise Henderson
1812-1851

Frederick Christian Havemeyer
1774-1841
m. Catharine Billiger
1784-1876

Susannah W. Havemeyer
1813-1856
m. Henry Senff
1804-1868

---

*   partial

John C. Havemeyer
1833-1922

Henry Havemeyer
1838-1886

Hector C. Havemeyer
1840-1889

James Havemeyer
1842-1912

Charles W. Havemeyer
1847-1895

William F. Havemeyer Jr.
1850-1913

Mary Osborne Havemeyer
1834-1865
m.
J. Lawrence Elder
1832-1868

George W. Havemeyer
1837-1861

Theodore A. Havemeyer
1839-1897

Henry O. Havemeyer
1847-1907
m. ——— Horace Havemeyer
Louisine W. Elder   1886-1956
1855-1929   m. Doris Dick
                     1890-1982

Charles H. Senff
1841-1911

Dick Family Tree

John Henry Dick
  b. 22 Feb 1851
  New York City
  d. 30 Sep 1925
  Islip, NY
  m. Nov 1886

Julia Theodora Mollenhauer
  (see Mollenhauer tree)

William Dick
  b. 24 Sep 1823
  Bruchhagen
  Hannover, Germany
  d. 5 Apr 1912
  Brooklyn NY
  m. 19 Nov 1848
  New York City

Anna Maria Vagts
  b. 2 Oct 1819
  Hanstedt, near Zeven
  Hannover, Germany
  d. 28 Feb 1898
  Brooklyn, NY

Anna Margaretha Dick
  b. 10 Feb 1861
  Brooklyn, NY
  d. 11 Oct 1935
  m. 2 Oct 1882
  no issue

J. Adolph Mollenhauer
  (see Mollenhauer tree)

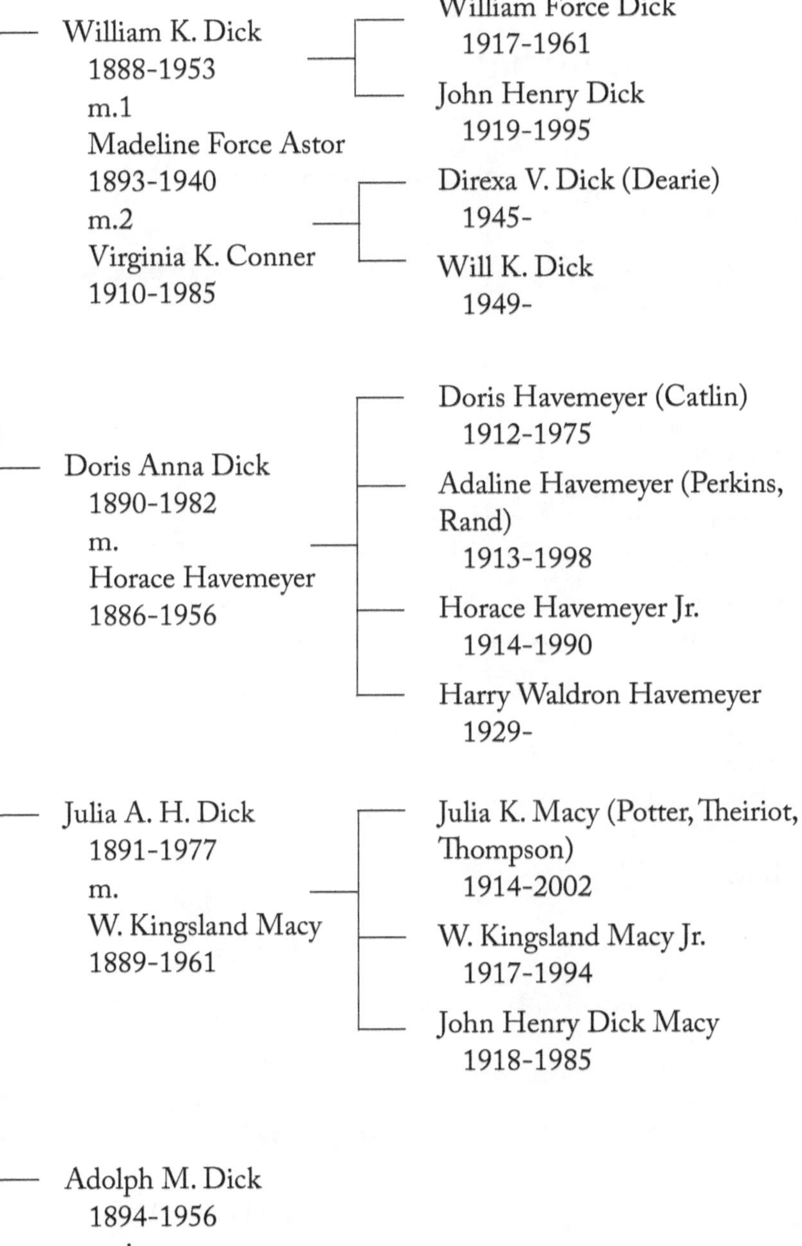

William K. Dick
1888-1953
m.1
Madeline Force Astor
1893-1940
m.2
Virginia K. Conner
1910-1985

William Force Dick
1917-1961

John Henry Dick
1919-1995

Direxa V. Dick (Dearie)
1945-

Will K. Dick
1949-

Doris Anna Dick
1890-1982
m.
Horace Havemeyer
1886-1956

Doris Havemeyer (Catlin)
1912-1975

Adaline Havemeyer (Perkins, Rand)
1913-1998

Horace Havemeyer Jr.
1914-1990

Harry Waldron Havemeyer
1929-

Julia A. H. Dick
1891-1977
m.
W. Kingsland Macy
1889-1961

Julia K. Macy (Potter, Theiriot, Thompson)
1914-2002

W. Kingsland Macy Jr.
1917-1994

John Henry Dick Macy
1918-1985

Adolph M. Dick
1894-1956
no issue

Mollenhauer Family Tree

John Mollenhauer
b. 13 Aug 1827
Ebersdorf
Hannover, Germany
d. 31 Dec 1904
Brooklyn NY
m. 1854
New York City

Doris Siems
b. 9 Apr 1830
Bremerivörde
Hannover, Germany
d. 19 Mar 1915
Brooklyn, NY

- J. William Mollenhauer
  1855-1912
  m. (div. 1890)
  Julia Margarethe Trebing
  1868-1933

- J. Adolph Mollenhauer
  1857-1926
  m.
  Anna Margaretha Dick
  1861-1935
  no issue

- J. Eldred Mollenhauer
  1858, died young

- Frederick D. Mollenhauer
  1860-1914
  m.
  May Craig
  1864-1939

- Julia Theodora Mollenhauer
  1863-1931
  m.
  John Henry Dick
  1851-1925

- Henry F. Mollenhauer
  1866-1931
  m.
  Sarah W. Howe
  1867-1949

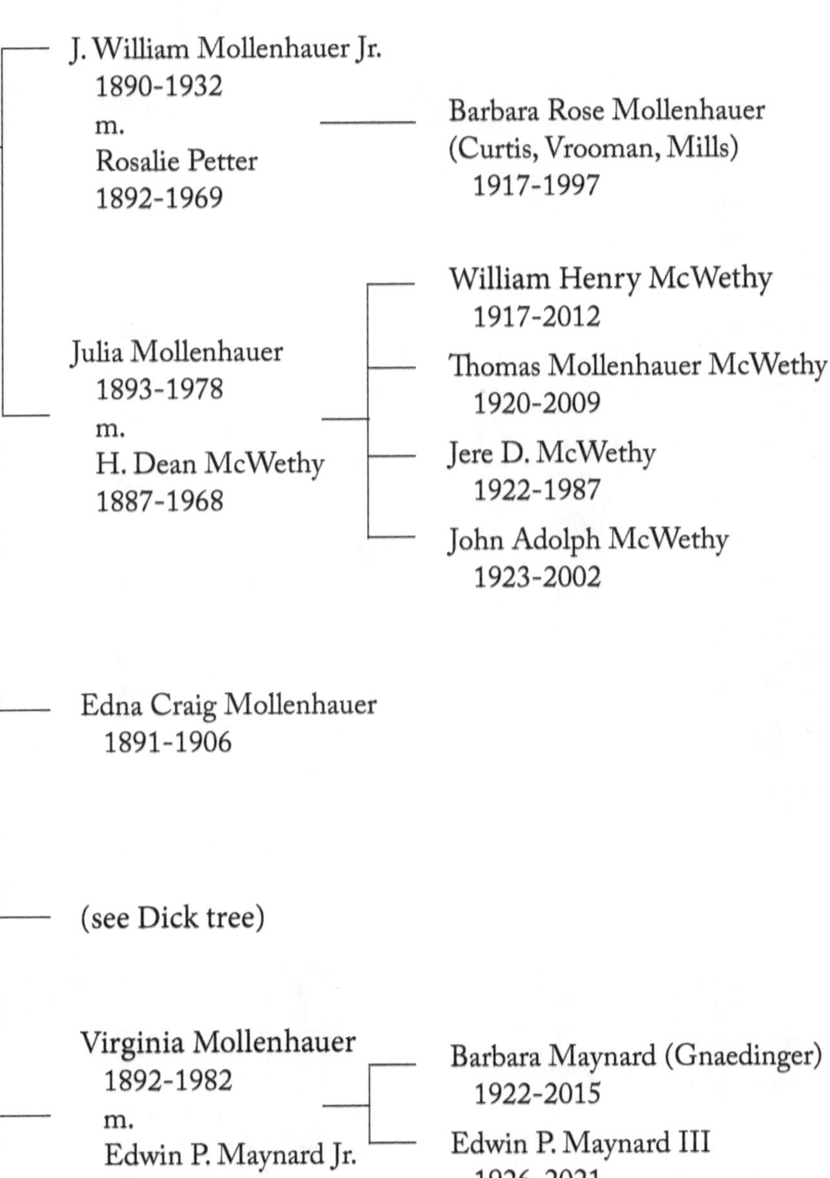

J. William Mollenhauer Jr.
1890-1932
m.
Rosalie Petter
1892-1969

Barbara Rose Mollenhauer
(Curtis, Vrooman, Mills)
1917-1997

Julia Mollenhauer
1893-1978
m.
H. Dean McWethy
1887-1968

William Henry McWethy
1917-2012

Thomas Mollenhauer McWethy
1920-2009

Jere D. McWethy
1922-1987

John Adolph McWethy
1923-2002

Edna Craig Mollenhauer
1891-1906

(see Dick tree)

Virginia Mollenhauer
1892-1982
m.
Edwin P. Maynard Jr.
1892-1984

Barbara Maynard (Gnaedinger)
1922-2015

Edwin P. Maynard III
1926-2021

APPENDIX D
American Sugar Refining Company
Board of Directors, 1891–1910[*]

1891	Henry O. Havemeyer, President	Theodore A. Havemeyer	F. O. Matthiessen	John E. Searles	Captain John B. Thomas	William Dick	George Magoun
1893					Washington B. Thomas		John E. Parsons
1897		Charles H. Senff[1]					
1898						John Mayer[2]	
1899				Lowell M. Palmer			
1900			Arthur Donner[3]				
1905				George H. Frazier[4]			
1907	Horace Havemeyer						
1908							
1910	resigned	resigned	resigned			resigned	resigned

[*] The board was made up of seven members until 1908, when two more were added: Henry C. Mott and Henry E. Niese
1 H. O. Havemeyer's cousin
2 Theodore A. Havemeyer's son-in-law
3 Brooklyn refiner
4 Philadelphia refiner

APPENDIX E
National Sugar Refining Company
Board of Directors, 1900–1912[*]

	James H. Post, President	F. D. Mollenhauer, Vice President and Treasurer	H. F. Mollenhauer, Assistant Treasurer	George D. Bunker, Secretary	Frederick H. Howell[1]	Herbert D. Cory[1]	Claus Doscher
1900	James H. Post, President	F. D. Mollenhauer, Vice President and Treasurer	H. F. Mollenhauer, Assistant Treasurer	George D. Bunker, Secretary	Frederick H. Howell[1]	Herbert D. Cory[1]	Claus Doscher
1901							J. Henry Dick
1904						Johannes Bruyn[2]	
1905 (Dec.)					Arthur Donner[3]	George H. Frazer[3]	John Mayer[3]
1910 (Jan.)					Thomas A. Howell[1]	Nathaniel Tooker	J. Henry Dick
1910 (April)					Charles J. Welch[4]		
1911 (April)					Thomas A. Howell[1]		
1912						Johannes Bruyn	resigned
	member until his death in 1938	member until his death in 1914	member until his death in 1931	member until his death in 1927	retired in 1930		

[*] The board was seven in number.
1 Partners of B. H. Howell Sons
2 Employee of B. H. Howell Sons
3 American Sugar Refining Company director designee
4 Horace Havemeyer designee

Havemeyers & Elder Refinery

The following description of the new refinery, filtering house, machine shop, cooperage and railroad depot, and other buildings connected with the Havemeyer [sic] & Elder establishment, we condense from the *Brooklyn Daily Eagle*, July 30, 1883.

The building, or buildings rather, for there are two of them—a refinery proper and a filtering house—are the largest of the kind on the face of the globe, and, when supplied with all the machinery, and in full operation, will have by far the largest capacity of any refinery on either continent.

The present monster structure furnishes an idea of the enormous business done by Mr. Havemeyer. His immense establishments, which cover so much of the Eastern District river front, are completed in all their appointments, with the addition of a new machine shop, which is now finished. The establishments of Mr. Havemeyer, connected with the new refinery, are bounded by South Second and South Sixth streets, First street and the East River. On the east side of First street, running midway in the block between South Third and South Fourth streets, is a great structure which was used as a boiler house and for filtering purposes, before the great fire a year and a half or more ago. The building is eleven stories high above ground, and had been connected by an iron bridge across First street at the third story with the burned buildings.

The buildings on the water front may be classed in this wise: On the block bounded by South Second and South Third streets, First street and the river, is the new refinery and filtering house, ten and thirteen stories in height respectively; on the block bounded by

South Third and South Fourth streets, First street and the river, a six-story structure has just been erected on the ruins of the old building. This structure will be used as a warehouse. Beside his great refining and storage establishments, Mr. Havemeyer controls the vast cooperage interests covering the large square bounded by First and Second streets, and North Fourth and North Fifth streets, which is familiarly known as Palmer's cooper shop. On the north side of North Fifth street, and bounded by First and Second streets, and running midway in the block between North Fifth and North Sixth streets, is Mr. Havemeyer's freight depot, which he placed at the exclusive use of the Erie Railroad. The other sugar refiners in that section of the city, and business men generally, ship and receive freight at this very important station of the Erie road. It is said that it ranks fourth in a business point of view among the freight depots of the road. The depot has become such an important one that it is now altogether too small, but no doubt Mr. Havemeyer will extend it and run the road a block further east. The trains are taken to and brought from Jersey City on barge floats several times during the day.

On the block bounded by South Fourth and South Fifth streets is a seven-story refinery, formerly used as a storage house, and on the block south of this structure is a one-story brick building used for storage purposes also. It is not in anyway connected with the building north of it. All the buildings are supposed to be fire-proof, only iron and brick being used in their construction. Three of the buildings will be connected at one of the upper stories by bridges.

In addition to these great buildings named, Mr. Havemeyer controls the refinery yet bearing the name of DeCastro & Donner, at the foot of South Ninth street and the establishment at the foot of North Third street. The latter building covers a large block, and the South Ninth street structure is also of giant proportions.

The new refinery stands upon a plot of ground, 250 x 150 feet, and consists of the refinery proper, which is 250 feet on First street and 70 feet deep, and the filtering house, which is 250 x 80 feet. The refinery is ten stories in height, or about 110 feet above ground, with a cellar depth of 20 feet, and the only materials used in its construction were pressed brick and iron. The walls are four feet in thickness at the bottom, and two feet at the top. The floors are of brick, being a series of flat topped arches of 5 feet sweep, and they are supported by a labyrinth of cast iron columns, and wrought iron beams and girders, which are braced to sixty-six cast iron columns, each capable of standing a strain of 400 tons. The courses and trimmings of the walls are of blue stone, and the mansard roof is faced with black brick. In order to make the building as absolutely fire-proof as possible, all material of an inflammable nature was eliminated in its construction. The entrance archways are secured with double iron doors, and the hundreds of windows are supplied with doors of the same material.

The whole premises are lighted by four hundred electric lights. No other light or fire of any kind is permitted in the buildings, as the furnaces are some distance back of both buildings, near the dock. There are hose pipes on each floor, and the buildings are supplied with fire escapes. It is claimed that the temperature can be kept down to 100 degrees in warm weather, on account of the perfect ventilation given by so many windows.

Back of the refinery, and separated from it by a fire wall, four feet thick, is the filtering house, the tallest building on the river front. The structure is 80 X 250 feet, and rises to an altitude of 150 feet, divided into thirteen stories. In architectural design it is similar to the refinery, the materials used being pressed brick and iron. The two upper stories are of black brick in the form of a mansard roof. On the river side of the filtering house is an immense chimney, 40 feet at the base and 200 feet high. Midway between the two buildings is a large well hole, extending to the roof and covered with a skylight.

This shaft gives both light and ventilation, as windows and doors open into it from the several floors. The windows and doors can be closed easily in the event of fire so as to prevent the spread of flames from one building to another.

In the rear of the filtering house is the boiler house, a two-story structure at the river. It is built on piles so as to resist the washing of the waves and tides, which might otherwise undermine the building and cause a caving in. Back of the boiler house is a new wharf. These buildings are constructed on a new plan suited to the improved machinery, with which they are supplied. There are 108 cast iron filters, 20 feet high by 9 feet interior diameter, which can be automatically filled and emptied, and there are six vacuum pans of 16 feet diameter, and twenty-four centrifugal machines of 64 feet diameter. The boilers are double decked, and similar to those of the Steam Heating Company of New York, and the elevating will be done by three Otis hoists. The boilers are of 4,000 horse power.

The capacity of the refinery is about 1,250,000 pounds of sugar daily. The estimated cost of the buildings and machinery is $2,500,000. The buildings will be connected with the warehouse on the south side by bridges crossing the street at the second and third stories.

On the ruins of the burned building has been erected an imposing, six-story, fire-proof structure, 180 x 150 feet. From this warehouse the material is rolled across the bridges to the refinery when required.

Back of the warehouse, and separated from it by a fireproof wall, is a machine shop, 180 x 75 feet, of fire-proof construction. It is supplied with the necessary facilities for keeping in repair the enormous amount of machinery used in the refinery.

Some Williamsburgh Street Names Assigned in 1885

Kent Avenue Chancellor James Kent, eminent New York jurist, who died in 1847.

Wythe Avenue George Wythe of Virginia, signer of the Declaration of Independence.

Berry Street Dr. Abraham J. Berry, the first mayor of Williamsburgh, 1852-53.

Bedford Avenue The anglicized form of the Dutch word Bestevaar, which is a translation of the Indian name of the locality, meaning the council place-where the wise men meet. Driggs Avenue Edmund Driggs, last village president elected in 1850, leading citizen and president of the Williamsburgh City Fire Insurance Company.

Roebling Street John A. Roebling, builder of the Brooklyn Bridge.

Havemeyer Street Frederick C. Havemeyer Jr., pioneer Williamsburgh sugar refiner.

Ross Street George Ross of Pennsylvania, signer of the Declaration of Independence.

Rush Street Benjamin Rush of Pennsylvania, signer of the Declaration of Independence.

MANHATTAN

1 The original Havemeyer Sugar Refinery
87-91 Vandam St.
2 Wintjen & Dick - Flour & Feed
West and Murray Sts.
3 St. Matthew's Lutheran Church
79 Walker St.
4 The first Dick home
Oak and Chestnut Sts.
5 The first Mollenhauer home
Eldridge and Hester Sts.
6 Wintjen Dick & Schumacher - Sugar Refinery
Pike and Cherry Sts.
7 Mollenhauer Wines and Liquors
Rutgers and Cherry Sts.
8 Mollenhauer Grocery Store
159 Walker St.

WILLIAMSBURG WATERFRONT

A Havemeyers & Elder Refinery
Kent Ave. (S. 2nd to S. 6th Sts.)
B Brooklyn Sugar Refinery
Kent Ave. (S. 2nd to S. 3rd Sts.)
C De Castro & Donner #2
Kent Ave. (N.2nd to N. 3rd Sts.)
Kent Ave. (N. 3rd to N. 4th Sts.)
D Dick & Meyer Refinery
Kent Ave. and N. 7th St.
E Havemeyer Sugar Refining Co.
Commercial St. (Greenpoint)
F Doscher Refinery - National Sugar
56th Ave. (Long Island City)
G Havemeyers & Elder Property
Brooklyn Eastern District Terminal
Kent Ave. (N. 5th to N. 10th Sts.)
H Wintjen, Dick & Schumacher
Kent Ave. and Division Ave.
I Mollenhauer Sugar Refinery
Kent Ave. and S. 11th St.
J Mollenhauer Molasses House
Rush St.
K De Castro & Donner #1 Refinery
Kent Ave. and S. 10th St.

WILLIAMSBURG INLAND

L Manufacturers National Bank
Broadway and Berry St.
M Dime Savings Bank of Williamsburgh
Broadway and Wythe Ave.
N Dick's last home
S. 9th St and Driggs Ave.
O Mollenhauer's last home
156 Ross St.
P Dick's home in "Dutchtown"
77 Union Ave.
Q Dick's church - St. John's
Maujer St. and Graham Ave.
R Mollenhauer's church - St. Peter's
Bedford and De Kalb Aves.
S Dime Savings Bank (present site)
Havemeyer St. (S. 5th St to S. 6th St.)
T Hanover Club
Bedford Ave. and Rodney St.
U Church of the Redeemer
Bedford Ave. and Hewes St.

DOWNTOWN BROOKLYN

V Arbuckle Sugar Refinery
Pearl and Jay Sts.
W Oxnard Brothers Refinery
Washington and Sands Sts.

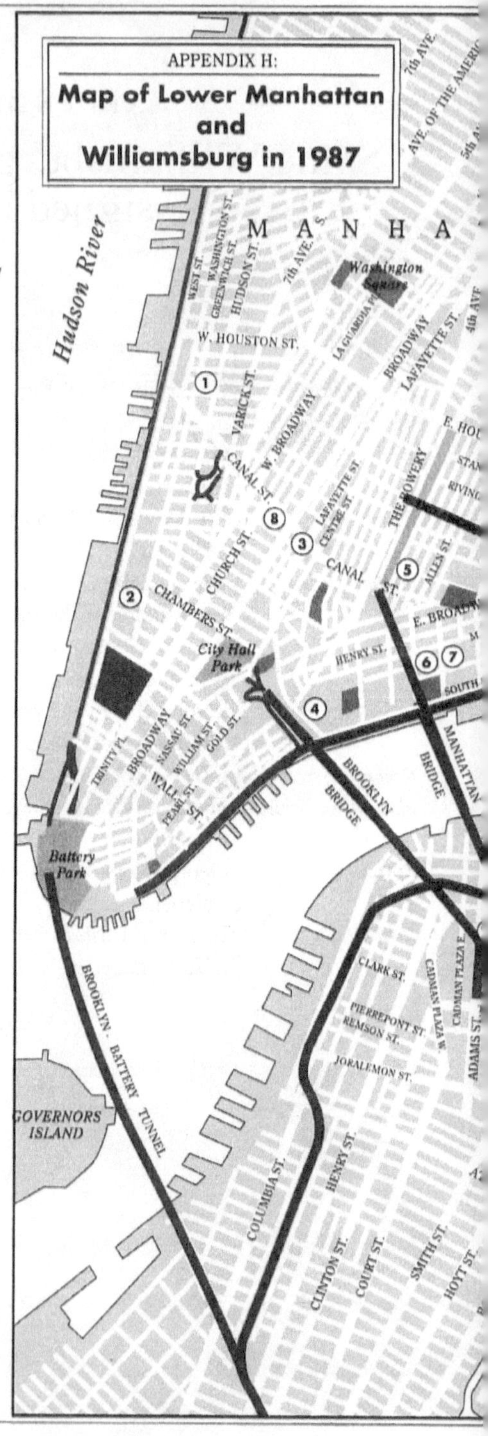

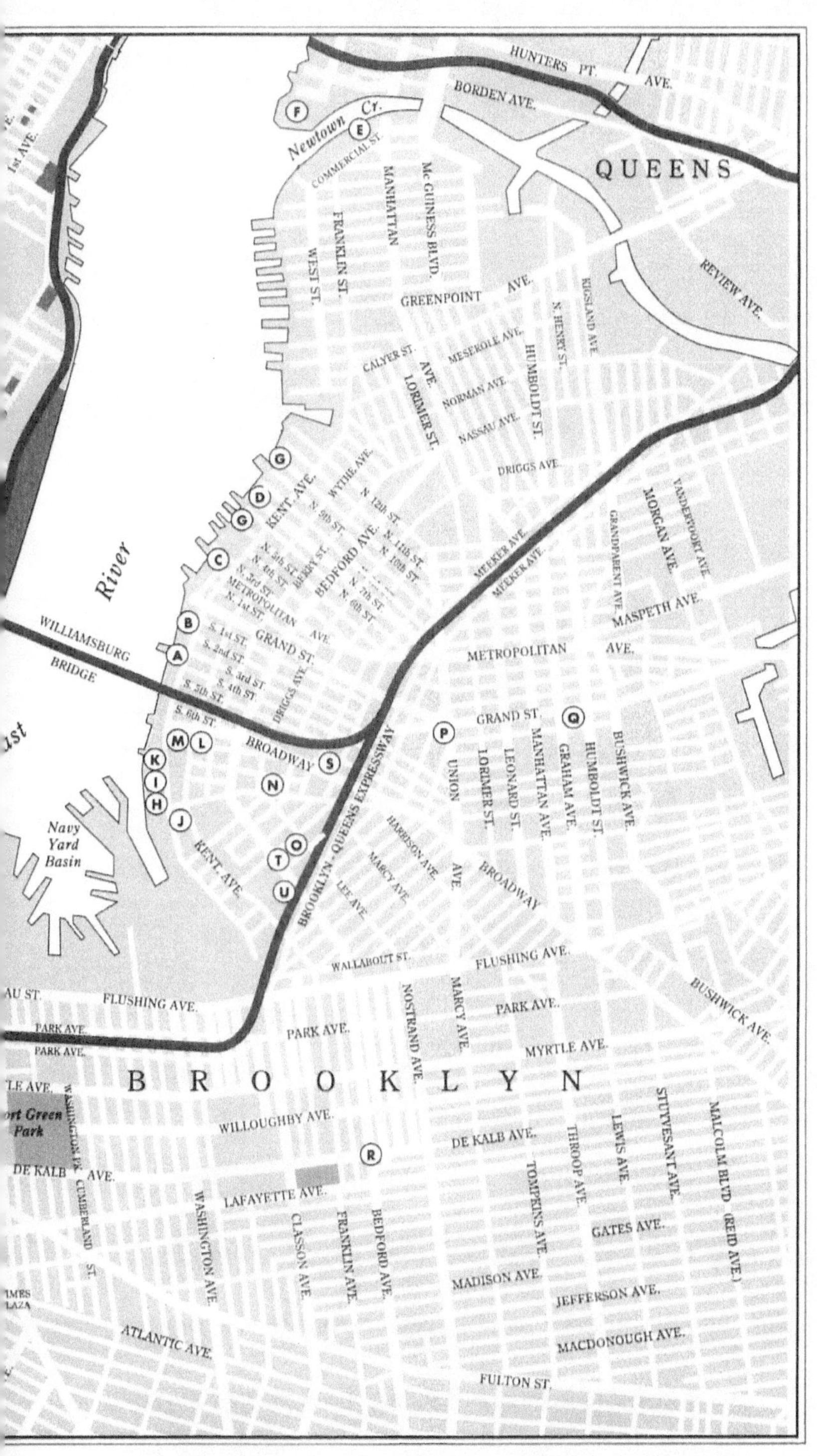

QUEENS
BROOKLYN
River
East
Navy Yard Basin
Fort Green Park
HUNTERS PT. AVE.
BORDEN AVE.
Newtown Cr.
COMMERCIAL ST.
MANHATTAN AVE.
McGUINESS BLVD.
GREENPOINT AVE.
FRANKLIN ST.
WEST ST.
CALYER ST.
MESEROLE AVE.
NORMAN AVE.
NASSAU AVE.
LORIMER ST.
HUMBOLDT ST.
N. HENRY ST.
KIOSLAND AVE.
REVIEW AVE.
DRIGGS AVE.
MORGAN AVE.
VANDERVOORT AVE.
GRANDPARENT AVE.
MEEKER AVE.
MEEKER AVE.
MASPETH AVE.
KENT AVE.
WYTHE AVE.
N. 12th ST.
N. 11th ST.
N. 10th ST.
N. 9th ST.
BERRY ST.
BEDFORD AVE.
N. 7th ST.
N. 6th ST.
N. 4th ST.
N. 3rd ST.
METROPOLITAN
N. 1st ST.
METROPOLITAN AVE.
GRAND ST.
S. 1st ST.
S. 2nd ST.
S. 3rd ST.
S. 4th ST.
S. 5th ST.
S. 6th ST.
WILLIAMSBURG BRIDGE
BROADWAY
KENT AVE.
BROOKLYN - QUEENS EXPRESSWAY
GRAND ST.
UNION AVE.
MANHATTAN AVE.
LEONARD ST.
LORIMER ST.
GRAHAM AVE.
HUMBOLDT ST.
BUSHWICK AVE.
BROADWAY
HARRISON AVE.
MARCY AVE.
LEE AVE.
WALLABOUT ST.
FLUSHING AVE.
BUSHWICK AVE.
NOSTRAND AVE.
MARCY AVE.
PARK AVE.
MYRTLE AVE.
FLUSHING AVE.
PARK AVE.
PARK AVE.
PARK AVE.
WILLOUGHBY AVE.
DE KALB AVE.
WASHINGTON AVE.
WASHINGTON PK.
CUMBERLAND ST.
DE KALB AVE.
LAFAYETTE AVE.
CLASSON AVE.
FRANKLIN AVE.
BEDFORD AVE.
MADISON AVE.
JEFFERSON AVE.
MACDONOUGH AVE.
THROOP AVE.
TOMPKINS AVE.
LEWIS AVE.
GATES AVE.
STUYVESANT AVE.
MALCOLM BLVD. (REID AVE.)
FULTON ST.
ATLANTIC AVE.
TIMES PLAZA
1st AVE.

Bibliography

Books and Articles

Annual Reports, Hanover Club, 1900, 1901, 1913

Armbruster, Eugene L. *Brooklyn's Eastern District*, 1942

Barbanel, Josh. "Domino Sugar Site Gets Makeover." *Wall Street Journal*, April 27, 2017

Brooklyn Register

Catlin, Daniel Jr. *Good Work Well Done*, New York: privately printed, 1988

Columbia Encyclopedia

Dime Savings Bank of Williamsburgh 50th Anniversary 1864-1914, 1914

Eichner, Alfred S. *The Emergency of Oligopoly: Sugar Refining as a Case Study*, 1966

Freeman, Joseph E. *A Century of Sugar Refining in the U.S.A. 1816-1916*, 1916

Hazelton, Henry Isham. *Boroughs of Brooklyn and Queens; Counties of Nassau and Suffolk*, 1925

History of the First German Evangelical Lutheran St. Peter's Church, 1913

Hoffman, Reverend Hugo W. Ph.D., pastor. *History of St. Paul's Evangelical Lutheran Church, Brooklyn, New York, 1853-1903*, 1903

Howard, Henry B. *The Eagle and Brooklyn: The Record of the Progress of the Brooklyn Daily Eagle; The History of the City of Brooklyn*, 1893

Laterman, Katya. "A New Tower Opens on the Domino Site in Williamsburg," *New York Times*, September 12, 2019

Lotkin, Roger W. *Brooklyn from the Civil War to the Great Renunciation*, 1985

Lienau, J. Henry. *A Description and History of an Early Day Sugar Refinery in New York*, 1938, 1944

Manhattan Register

Mullin, Jack Simpson. *The Sugar Trust: Henry O. Havemeyer and the American Sugar Refining Company*, 1964

Stiles, Henry Reed, ed. *The History of Kings County*, 1884
    a. Brockett, L. P., M.D. "The Manufacturing Industries"
    b. Brockett, L. P., M.D. "Early History of Williamsburgh"

c. Brockett, L. P., M.D. "Banking of Williamsburgh"
d. "Cooperage of Williamsburgh"
e. "Churches of Williamsburgh"
Vogt, Paul L. Ph.D. *The Sugar Refining Industry in the United States*, 1908

Public Documents

Norman B. Tooker et al. v . National Sugar Refining Company and Others, in
    Chancery of New Jersey, filed January 31, 1911
Original Petition: US. v. A.S.R.C., filed November 28, 1910, also minutes
    thereof
Report and Proceedings of the Joint Committee of the Senate and Assembly of
    the State of New York, Senator Lexow, Chairman, 1897
U.S. House of Representatives, Special Committee on the Investigation of the
    American Sugar Refining Company and Others. Rep. Hardwick,
    Chairman, 1911-12
        Hardwick Committee—Hearings, 1911
        Hardwick Committee—Report
US. Industrial Commission Reports, 1900-1902

Private Papers and Documents

Documents regarding Havemeyers & Elder and the Brooklyn Eastern District
    Terminal in possession of Harry W. Havemeyer
Documents regarding the estate of William Dick in possession of Harry W.
    Havemeyer
Dunham, Carl J. *History of Havemeyer to Amstar, Update Domino Sugar*, 2002
Havemeyer, Henry O. *Biographic Record of the Havemeyer Family*, 1944
Maynard, Edwin P. *John Mollenhauer and His Descendants: A Genealogy*, 1981
Various documents relating to the families of William Dick and John
    Mollenhauer in the possession of Direxa Dick Dearie

Newspapers

Brooklyn Citizen, October 29, 1916
Brooklyn Daily Eagle
    July 30, 1883
    April 20, 1914
    January 1, 1905

April 6, 1912
June 21, 1925
Brooklyn Times, December 11, 1897
Brooklyn Times Union, April 8, 1934
Islip Herald, April 6, 1912
New York Times
December 16, 1889
July 3, 1891
July 29, 1891
April 17, 1900
January 1, 1905
October 15, 1910
April 6, 1912
October 1, 1915
July 6, 1919
March 6, 1938
Williamsburgh Times, September 14, 1848

Maps and Atlases

Atlas of Long Island, New York
Map of 1873 by F. W. Beers, published by Beers, Comstock & Cline, 36 Vesey
    Street, New York, NY
Map of Williamsburgh, 1852
Maps of the Eastern District of Brooklyn by Sanborn Map Company, 1887,
    1904-5

Photographs

Album of photographs of factories owned by the American Sugar Refining
    Company, 1911
Engraving of Williamsburgh, Long Island, from Whitefield's *Original Views of
    North American Cities*, 1852
Photographs of Eastern District buildings from *King's Views of Brooklyn*, 1905
Family photographs in the possession of Harry W. Havemeyer